# The Best Of *Teacher's Helper*®
## Reproducibles And Activities For Your Classroom
# Math
## Grades 2–3

### Editor in Chief
Margaret Michel

### Manager, Product Development
Charlotte Perkins

### Manager, Magazines Division
Julie Peck

### Editors
Jennifer L. Overend
Kathy Wolf

### Contributing Writers
Diane Badden, Lorie Bruce, Valerie Burns, Janice Bradley Gislason,
Valerie Lathrop, Sarah McCutcheon, Beth Schimmel

### Copy Editor
Debbie Blaylock

### Artists
Jennifer T. Bennett, Pam Crane, Teresa Davidson, Lucia Kemp Henry, Susan Hodnett,
Barry Slate, Rebecca Saunders, Donna Teal

### Cover Artist
Cathy Spangler Bruce

### Typographer
Lynette Maxwell

# Table Of Contents

Name _____

# Off-Road Racers

How fast can these off-road racers go?
Have your partners time you.
Write each time in the space.

**Hint:**
The lowest time is the fastest!

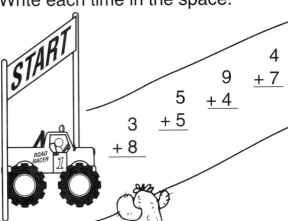

$$\begin{array}{r} 3 \\ +8 \\ \hline \end{array}$$
$$\begin{array}{r} 5 \\ +5 \\ \hline \end{array}$$
$$\begin{array}{r} 9 \\ +4 \\ \hline \end{array}$$
$$\begin{array}{r} 4 \\ +7 \\ \hline \end{array}$$
$$\begin{array}{r} 2 \\ +8 \\ \hline \end{array}$$
$$\begin{array}{r} 7 \\ +9 \\ \hline \end{array}$$
$$\begin{array}{r} 8 \\ +9 \\ \hline \end{array}$$
$$\begin{array}{r} 7 \\ +7 \\ \hline \end{array}$$
$$\begin{array}{r} 9 \\ +6 \\ \hline \end{array}$$
$$\begin{array}{r} 5 \\ +7 \\ \hline \end{array}$$
$$\begin{array}{r} 7 \\ +6 \\ \hline \end{array}$$
$$\begin{array}{r} 4 \\ +8 \\ \hline \end{array}$$

Time: _____

$$\begin{array}{r} 9 \\ +8 \\ \hline \end{array}$$
$$\begin{array}{r} 6 \\ +9 \\ \hline \end{array}$$
$$\begin{array}{r} 5 \\ +8 \\ \hline \end{array}$$
$$\begin{array}{r} 9 \\ +9 \\ \hline \end{array}$$
$$\begin{array}{r} 5 \\ +9 \\ \hline \end{array}$$
$$\begin{array}{r} 3 \\ +7 \\ \hline \end{array}$$
$$\begin{array}{r} 6 \\ +5 \\ \hline \end{array}$$
$$\begin{array}{r} 8 \\ +3 \\ \hline \end{array}$$
$$\begin{array}{r} 6 \\ +2 \\ \hline \end{array}$$
$$\begin{array}{r} 6 \\ +6 \\ \hline \end{array}$$
$$\begin{array}{r} 8 \\ +7 \\ \hline \end{array}$$
$$\begin{array}{r} 2 \\ +4 \\ \hline \end{array}$$

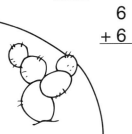

Time: _____

$$\begin{array}{r} 8 \\ +6 \\ \hline \end{array}$$
$$\begin{array}{r} 4 \\ +3 \\ \hline \end{array}$$
$$\begin{array}{r} 7 \\ +8 \\ \hline \end{array}$$
$$\begin{array}{r} 7 \\ +3 \\ \hline \end{array}$$
$$\begin{array}{r} 9 \\ +3 \\ \hline \end{array}$$
$$\begin{array}{r} 8 \\ +2 \\ \hline \end{array}$$
$$\begin{array}{r} 5 \\ +3 \\ \hline \end{array}$$
$$\begin{array}{r} 4 \\ +4 \\ \hline \end{array}$$
$$\begin{array}{r} 9 \\ +2 \\ \hline \end{array}$$
$$\begin{array}{r} 8 \\ +8 \\ \hline \end{array}$$
$$\begin{array}{r} 4 \\ +9 \\ \hline \end{array}$$
$$\begin{array}{r} 4 \\ +5 \\ \hline \end{array}$$

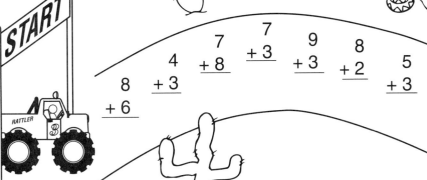

Use the answer key to check your answers.
For each incorrect answer, add one second to
 your time in that race.
If all answers are correct, subtract three
 seconds from your time in that race.

Time: _____

# How To Use This Unit

Students work together to increase math-fact speed and accuracy with this fun unit. Duplicate pages 3, 5, and 7 for each of your students. Then divide your students into pairs. Have students take turns timing one another on each of the reproducible activities. Make several answer keys available to your students for checking their work. Explain to your students the importance of not only solving the facts quickly, but also arriving at the correct answers. Use this unit later in the school year to test your youngsters' progress.

**Answer Key**

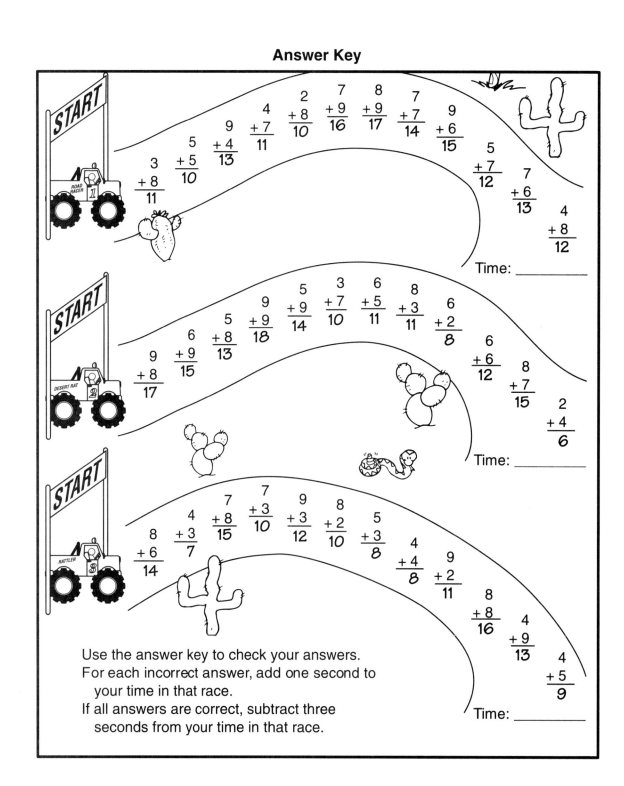

Use the answer key to check your answers.
For each incorrect answer, add one second to your time in that race.
If all answers are correct, subtract three seconds from your time in that race.

Name _____

# Ready, Set, Go!

How fast can each car go?
Have your partner time you.
Write your time at the end of each race.

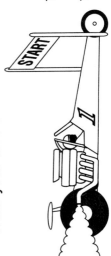

**Car 1 (START)**

12 − 5 = _____    10 − 8 = _____    9 − 2 = _____    10 − 3 = _____    11 − 7 = _____    14 − 6 = _____

13 − 8 = _____    14 − 9 = _____    8 − 3 = _____    12 − 3 = _____    16 − 9 = _____    15 − 7 = _____

Time: _____

**Car 2 (START)**

13 − 7 = _____    11 − 6 = _____    16 − 8 = _____    12 − 4 = _____    10 − 6 = _____    11 − 8 = _____

18 − 9 = _____    14 − 7 = _____    9 − 3 = _____    11 − 9 = _____    15 − 6 = _____    8 − 2 = _____

Time: _____

**Car 3 (START)**

12 − 9 = _____    14 − 5 = _____    9 − 5 = _____    17 − 9 = _____    12 − 5 = _____    15 − 8 = _____

13 − 5 = _____    12 − 8 = _____    8 − 5 = _____    13 − 4 = _____    10 − 4 = _____    11 − 5 = _____

Time: _____

**Car 4 (START)**

13 − 6 = _____    15 − 9 = _____    12 − 6 = _____    8 − 4 = _____    11 − 3 = _____    10 − 5 = _____

14 − 8 = _____    9 − 4 = _____    11 − 2 = _____    17 − 8 = _____    13 − 9 = _____    16 − 7 = _____

Time: _____

Use an answer key to check your answers.
For each incorrect answer, add one second to that car's time.
If all answers are correct, subtract three seconds from that car's time!

Which cars finished first, second, third, and fourth?
Write each car's number on the correct line.

1st place: Car # _____      3rd place: Car # _____

2nd place: Car # _____      4th place: Car # _____

# Extension Activity
## Fact Memorization

Motivate students to memorize their math facts with these fun cards. Duplicate a supply of the cards on page 8 for each child. Have students cut out, color, and program their cards. Have students code the backs of the cards with the answers. Give each child a plastic baggie in which to store his cards. Encourage children to use their cards at home for speedy fact memorization.

## Answer Key

| | | | | | |
|---|---|---|---|---|---|
| 12 − 5 = 7 | 10 − 8 = 2 | 9 − 2 = 7 | 10 − 3 = 7 | 11 − 7 = 4 | 14 − 6 = 8 |
| 13 − 8 = 5 | 14 − 9 = 5 | 8 − 3 = 5 | 12 − 3 = 9 | 16 − 9 = 7 | 15 − 7 = 8 |

| | | | | | |
|---|---|---|---|---|---|
| 13 − 7 = 6 | 11 − 6 = 5 | 16 − 8 = 8 | 12 − 4 = 8 | 10 − 6 = 4 | 11 − 8 = 3 |
| 18 − 9 = 9 | 14 − 7 = 7 | 9 − 3 = 6 | 11 − 9 = 2 | 15 − 6 = 9 | 8 − 2 = 6 |

| | | | | | |
|---|---|---|---|---|---|
| 12 − 9 = 3 | 14 − 5 = 9 | 9 − 5 = 4 | 17 − 9 = 8 | 12 − 5 = 7 | 15 − 8 = 7 |
| 13 − 5 = 8 | 12 − 8 = 4 | 8 − 5 = 3 | 13 − 4 = 9 | 10 − 4 = 6 | 11 − 5 = 6 |

| | | | | | |
|---|---|---|---|---|---|
| 13 − 6 = 7 | 15 − 9 = 6 | 12 − 6 = 6 | 8 − 4 = 4 | 11 − 3 = 8 | 10 − 5 = 5 |
| 14 − 8 = 6 | 9 − 4 = 5 | 11 − 2 = 9 | 17 − 8 = 9 | 13 − 9 = 4 | 16 − 7 = 9 |

Name _____

# The Right-Of-Way Relay

Begin at the starting line and race to the end!
Have your partner time you for each leg of the race.
Write each time on the line.
Be sure to follow the + and – signs.

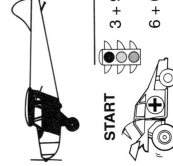

**START**

$3 + 9 =$ _____     $7 + 6 =$ _____     $6 + 7 =$ _____     $9 + 3 =$ _____     $9 + 9 =$ _____

$6 + 6 =$ _____     $9 + 4 =$ _____     $4 + 8 =$ _____     $8 + 3 =$ _____     $8 + 6 =$ _____     $4 + 5 =$ _____

$9 + 7 =$ _____

$13 - 4 =$ _____

**Time for 1st leg:** _____

$11 - 6 =$ _____     $15 - 6 =$ _____     $14 - 6 =$ _____     $17 - 8 =$ _____     $10 - 3 =$ _____     $14 - 7 =$ _____

$13 - 8 =$ _____     $12 - 3 =$ _____     $15 - 8 =$ _____     $12 - 4 =$ _____     $16 - 7 =$ _____

**Time for 2nd leg:** _____

$8 + 2 =$ _____     $7 + 8 =$ _____     $8 + 8 =$ _____     $9 + 5 =$ _____     $9 + 6 =$ _____     $6 + 5 =$ _____

$11 - 8 =$ _____     $16 - 9 =$ _____     $12 - 9 =$ _____     $14 - 5 =$ _____     $17 - 9 =$ _____     $11 - 2 =$ _____

**Time for 3rd leg:** _____

Total race
time:

_____

Use an answer key to check your answers.
For each incorrect answer, add one second to the time for that leg.
If all answers are correct, subtract three seconds from the time for that leg.
Find your total race time.

# Fact Cards

Use with the extension activity on page 6.

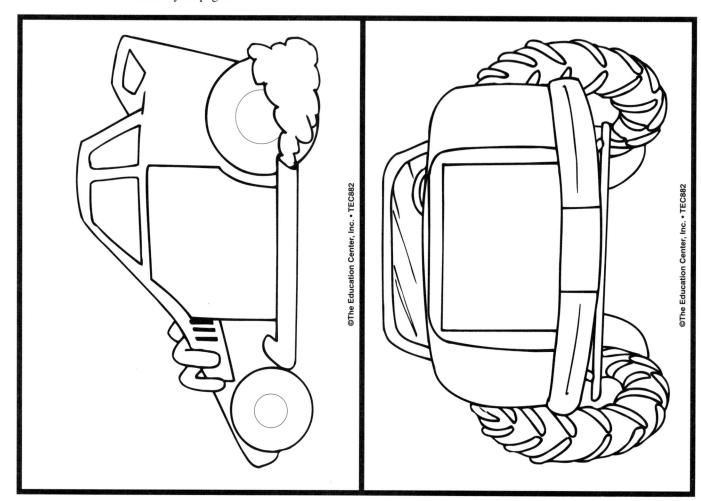

## Answer Key

| | | | | | |
|---|---|---|---|---|---|
| 3 + 9 = __12__ | 9 + 4 = __13__ | 7 + 6 = __13__ | 6 + 7 = __13__ | 9 + 3 = __12__ | 9 + 9 = __18__ |
| 6 + 6 = __12__ | 9 + 7 = __16__ | 4 + 8 = __12__ | 8 + 3 = __11__ | 8 + 6 = __14__ | 4 + 5 = __9__ |

Time

| | | | | | |
|---|---|---|---|---|---|
| 11 − 6 = __5__ | 15 − 6 = __9__ | 14 − 6 = __8__ | 17 − 8 = __9__ | 10 − 3 = __7__ | 14 − 7 = __7__ |
| 13 − 4 = __9__ | 13 − 8 = __5__ | 12 − 3 = __9__ | 15 − 8 = __7__ | 12 − 4 = __8__ | 16 − 7 = __9__ |

leg:

| | | | | | |
|---|---|---|---|---|---|
| 8 + 2 = __10__ | 7 + 8 = __15__ | 8 + 8 = __16__ | 9 + 5 = __14__ | 9 + 6 = __15__ | 6 + 5 = __11__9 |
| 11 − 8 = __3__ | 16 − 9 = __7__ | 12 − 9 = __3__ | 14 − 5 = __9__ | 17 − 9 = __8__ | 11 − 2 = _____ |

Name _____

# Pasta Dishes

Put 9 or less pasta pieces on one pot.
Put 9 or less pasta pieces on the other pot.
Count to find the total number of pieces.
Write the matching addition fact on a dish.
Fill each dish with a different addition fact.

# Materials Needed For Each Student

— 18 pasta pieces *or* 18 reproducible pasta pieces (below)
— pasta-pot manipulatives holder (optional, page 14)

# How To Use Page 9

Duplicate page 9 for each student. Have students manipulate their pasta pieces to illustrate addition facts having addends of nine or less. Then have the students write each matching math fact on a dish. Have students continue illustrating different math facts until all of their dishes are filled.

# How To Use The Manipulatives Below

Duplicate a set of manipulatives on white construction paper for each child. Have each child color and cut out his manipulative pasta pieces along the dotted lines. Students use the pasta manipulatives with the activities on pages 9, 11, and 13.

## Manipulative Pasta Pieces

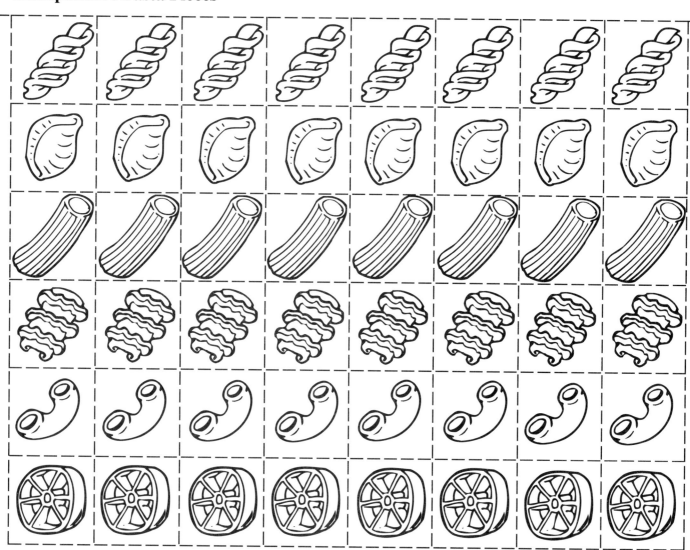

©The Education Center, Inc. • TEC882

## Answer Key

Answers will vary, but a different math fact (having addends of nine or less) should be written on each dish.

## "Pas-taah!"

Read the sum on a pasta box.

Fill the platter with a matching number of pasta pieces.

Divide the pieces into two sets of 9 or less each.

Write the matching addition fact on the box.

Fill each box with different facts.

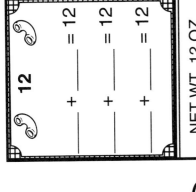

**12**

___ + ___ = 12

___ + ___ = 12

___ + ___ = 12

NET WT. 12 OZ.

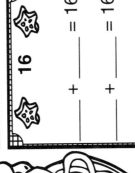

**16**

___ + ___ = 16

___ + ___ = 16

___ + ___ = 16

NET WT. 16 OZ.

**14**

___ + ___ = 14

___ + ___ = 14

___ + ___ = 14

NET WT. 14 OZ.

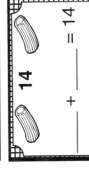

**17**

___ + ___ = 17

NET WT. 17 OZ.

**18**

___ + ___ = 18

NET WT. 18 OZ.

**13**

___ + ___ = 13

___ + ___ = 13

___ + ___ = 13

NET WT. 13 OZ.

**10**

___ + ___ = 10

___ + ___ = 10

___ + ___ = 10

NET WT. 10 OZ.

**11**

___ + ___ = 11

___ + ___ = 11

___ + ___ = 11

NET WT. 11 OZ.

**15**

___ + ___ = 15

___ + ___ = 15

___ + ___ = 15

NET WT. 15 OZ.

## Materials Needed For Each Student

— 18 pasta pieces *or* 18 reproducible pasta pieces (page 10)
— pasta-pot manipulatives holder (optional, page 14)

## How To Use Page 11

Duplicate page 11 for each student. Have students place the indicated number of pasta pieces on their platters, then divide the pasta into two sets that each have nine pieces or less. Next have the students write corresponding addition facts on their matching pasta boxes.

**Answer Key**

The addends written on each pasta box will vary, but their sums should equal the sum programmed on that box. All facts for each sum should be different.

# Pasta Plus

| 0 | 1 | 2 | 3 | 4 |
|---|---|---|---|---|
| 5 | 6 | 7 | 8 | 9 |
| 9 | 10 | 11 | 12 | 13 |
| 14 | 15 | 16 | 17 | 18 |

| 0 | 1 | 2 | 3 | 4 |
|---|---|---|---|---|
| 5 | 6 | 7 | 8 | 9 |

## Materials Needed For Each Student

— 40 pieces of pasta (20 each of two different shapes)
— zippered, plastic bag

## How To Use Page 13

Provide students with pasta pieces and construction-paper copies of page 13. If desired, have students color their gameboards. Divide the class into student pairs. To play, each student pair needs only *one* set of game components. Work through the directions, having student pairs manipulate their own game pieces. Once the student pairs understand the game rules, play may continue on their own. Have students store their pasta pieces and gameboards in zippered, plastic bags. Encourage students to take their games home for further practice.

## How To Use The Pasta Pot Below

Duplicate the pasta-pot pattern on construction paper for each child. Have the child color, cut out, and fold the pot pattern and staple or glue the sides of the pot together. Have the child store her manipulative pasta pieces (page 10) inside the pot.

## Pasta-Pot Pattern

## Directions For Two Players

1. Sort the pasta shapes. Player 1 uses one set of shapes as his markers. Player 2 uses the other set of shapes as his markers.
2. Player 1 places a piece of pasta on any number on the plate.
3. Player 2 places a piece of pasta on any number on the plate. (Note: Both pieces may be placed on the same number.)
4. Player 2 adds the two numbers that are covered (using pasta pieces as counters if necessary) and places a pasta piece on the pot to cover the matching sum.
5. Player 1 moves his pasta piece to a different number on the plate.
6. Player 1 adds the two numbers that are covered (using pasta pieces as counters if necessary) and places a pasta piece on the pot to cover the matching sum.
7. Play continues in this manner with each player moving his pasta piece on the plate, adding the two covered numbers, and placing a second pasta piece on the pot to cover the matching sum.
8. The winner is the first student to cover three squares in a row (vertically, horizontally, or diagonally) on the gameboard. **Hint:** Encourage students to play defensively to block their opponents.

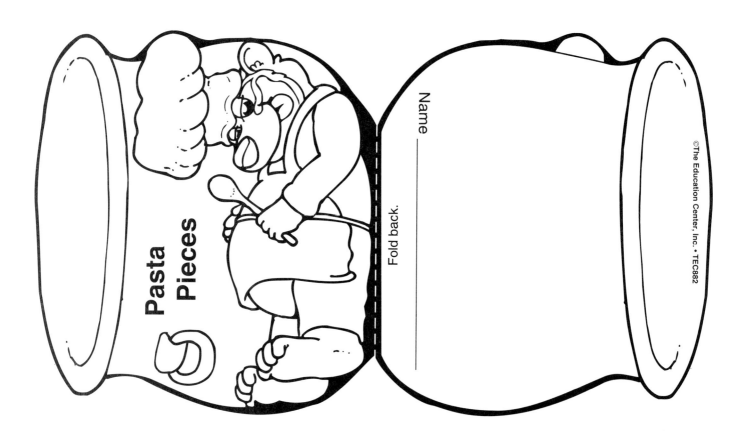

Name _____

# That's "Sum" Sandwich!

Solve the problems.

```
  54       73       64       44       60       39       33       17       58       25
+ 44     + 13     + 12     + 50     + 23     + 40     + 34     + 60     + 11     + 31
```

```
  23       60       57                37       82       25
+ 26     + 32     + 22              + 21     + 16     + 63
```

```
  51       13       42       12       62       45       35       76
+ 35     + 14     + 26     + 74     + 23     + 12     + 24     + 23
```

**Bonus Box:** On the back of this sheet, describe your favorite kind of sandwich. Color a picture of it.

15

## Background For The Teacher
## The Invention Of The Sandwich

John Montague was an English nobleman known as the Earl of Sandwich. He loved to play cards with his friends. In fact, Montague would often forego eating to continue his card playing. Once, after playing cards for 24 hours without a break, Montague ordered sliced meats and cheeses to be placed between two pieces of bread. This invention, which is now called the sandwich, allowed Montague to eat with one hand and continue to play cards with the other! The earliest sandwiches often contained a combination of foods traditionally found on a nobleman's table, such as bread, meat, greens, cheese, and onions. Today the sandwich is one of the most popular meals.

## Extension Activity
## Sandwich Party

Celebrate Sandwich Day on November 3 with a sandwich party lunch. Duplicate the parent note on page 18 for each of your students' parents. Have each child bring a different sandwich ingredient to contribute, such as different kinds of breads, jellies, meats, cheeses, condiments, vegetables, or peanut butter. On your Sandwich Day, allow each child to choose his desired ingredients and create his own sandwich. While students are eating, ask them to tell the ingredients used in their sandwiches. Have the students determine:

— how many children chose exactly the same ingredients
— which child used the most ingredients in his sandwich
— which child used the fewest ingredients in his sandwich
— which children created sandwiches they had never eaten before

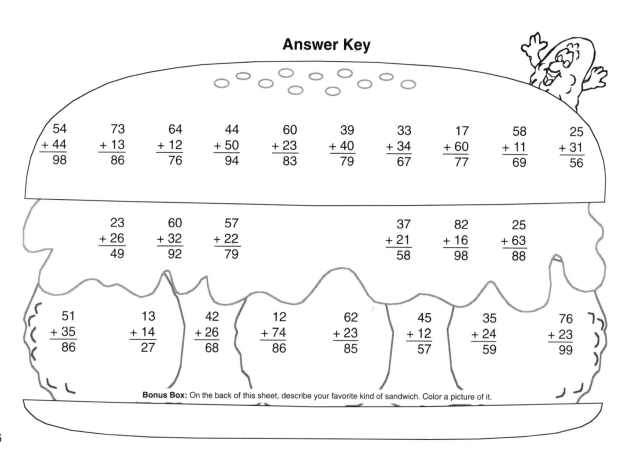

**Answer Key**

| | | | | | | | | | |
|---|---|---|---|---|---|---|---|---|---|
| 54 +44 = 98 | 73 +13 = 86 | 64 +12 = 76 | 44 +50 = 94 | 60 +23 = 83 | 39 +40 = 79 | 33 +34 = 67 | 17 +60 = 77 | 58 +11 = 69 | 25 +31 = 56 |

| 23 +26 = 49 | 60 +32 = 92 | 57 +22 = 79 | | 37 +21 = 58 | 82 +16 = 98 | 25 +63 = 88 |
|---|---|---|---|---|---|---|

| 51 +35 = 86 | 13 +14 = 27 | 42 +26 = 68 | 12 +74 = 86 | 62 +23 = 85 | 45 +12 = 57 | 35 +24 = 59 | 76 +23 = 99 |
|---|---|---|---|---|---|---|---|

**Bonus Box:** On the back of this sheet, describe your favorite kind of sandwich. Color a picture of it.

Name _____

# A Real "Mathful"

Solve the problems.
Show your work.

● 6    ● 8    ● 10

● 4

● 12

● 2

| 45 | 64 | 23 | 39 |
|----|----|----|----|
| + 27 | + 16 | + 28 | + 46 |

● 14

★ 0

● 48

| 51 | 46 | 15 | 48 |
|----|----|----|----|
| + 39 | + 26 | + 78 | + 27 |

● 16

● 18

● 46

| 17 | 58 | 44 | 53 |
|----|----|----|----|
| + 79 | + 16 | + 18 | + 27 |

● 20

● 44

| 64 | 78 | 36 | 21 |
|----|----|----|----|
| + 27 | + 19 | + 55 | + 49 |

● 22

● 42

● 24

| 16 | 57 | 26 | 33 |
|----|----|----|----|
| + 79 | + 36 | + 17 | + 29 |

● 40

● 26

● 30

● 38    ● 34    ● 28

● 32

● 36

Count by twos to connect the dots.

**Bonus Box:** Color your favorite sandwich fillings showing from the edges of the sandwich.

©The Education Center, Inc. • TEC882

17

# Parent Note

Use with the extension activity on page 16.

Dear Parent,

We will be having a sandwich party lunch on

_____ , _____ .
day                                    date

You can help by contributing the following sandwich

item: _____ .

Your child will not need to bring or purchase a lunch

on that day. Please sign and return the form below.

Thank you!

Sincerely,

_____
teacher signature

Yes! I will contribute _____

to the sandwich party.

_____
parent signature

**Answer Key**

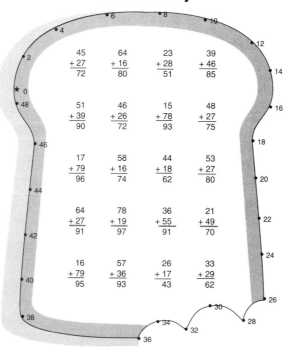

| | | | |
|---|---|---|---|
| 45<br>+ 27<br>72 | 64<br>+ 16<br>80 | 23<br>+ 28<br>51 | 39<br>+ 46<br>85 |
| 51<br>+ 39<br>90 | 46<br>+ 26<br>72 | 15<br>+ 78<br>93 | 48<br>+ 27<br>75 |
| 17<br>+ 79<br>96 | 58<br>+ 16<br>74 | 44<br>+ 18<br>62 | 53<br>+ 27<br>80 |
| 64<br>+ 27<br>91 | 78<br>+ 19<br>97 | 36<br>+ 55<br>91 | 21<br>+ 49<br>70 |
| 16<br>+ 79<br>95 | 57<br>+ 36<br>93 | 26<br>+ 17<br>43 | 33<br>+ 29<br>62 |

Name _____    Adding money: 2-digit, no regrouping

# Check, Please!

Use the menu to solve the problems on the order slips below.
The first one is done for you.

| | |
|---|---|
| Sprouts & Pickle<br>  Sandwich       32¢<br>Onion Rings    + 37¢<br>     total:    ⎯⎯⎯<br>              69¢ | Turkey & Banana<br>  Sandwich<br>Sprouts & Pickle<br>  Sandwich    + ⎯⎯⎯<br>     total: |
| Raisin & Relish<br>  Sandwich<br>Lemonade    + ⎯⎯⎯<br>     total: | Hot Fudge Roast<br>  Beef Sandwich<br>Potato Chips    + ⎯⎯⎯<br>     total: |
| French Fries<br><br>Milk    + ⎯⎯⎯<br>     total: | Ham & Jam<br>  Sandwich<br>Lemonade    + ⎯⎯⎯<br>     total: |
| Ham & Jam<br>  Sandwich<br>Potato Chips    + ⎯⎯⎯<br>     total: | Onion Rings<br><br>Milk    + ⎯⎯⎯<br>     total: |
| Peanut Butter &<br>  Tuna Sandwich<br>Lemonade    + ⎯⎯⎯<br>     total: | Lemonade<br><br>Milk    + ⎯⎯⎯<br>     total: |
| French Fries<br>Potato Chips    + ⎯⎯⎯<br>     total: | Onion Rings<br>Raisin & Relish<br>  Sandwich    + ⎯⎯⎯<br>     total: |

## How To Use Page 19

Duplicate copies of page 19 and the menu on this page for your students. Have the student look at each order slip, record the prices from the menu, add to determine the total cost, and record the total on the order slip.

For added fun, have each child cut apart her order slips when her page is complete and staple them together into an order pad. To extend the activity, have each student cut and staple writing paper into another order pad. Then have the child use the menu to create different food combinations to add.

# Silly Sandwich Shop Menu

## Sandwiches
Peanut Butter And Tuna ........................... 64¢

Ham And Jam ..................................... 75¢

Turkey And Banana ................................ 53¢

Raisin And Relish ................................ 41¢

Hot Fudge Roast Beef ............................. 86¢

Sprouts And Pickle ............................... 32¢

## Side Orders
Onion Rings ...................................... 37¢

French Fries ..................................... 28¢

Potato Chips ..................................... 11¢

## Drinks
Lemonade ......................................... 23¢

Milk ............................................. 31¢

## Answer Key

| | | | | |
|---|---|---|---|---|
| Sprouts & Pickle Sandwich | 32¢ | | Turkey & Banana Sandwich | 53¢ |
| Onion Rings | + 37¢ | | Sprouts & Pickle Sandwich | + 32¢ |
| total: | 69¢ | | total: | 85¢ |
| Raisin & Relish Sandwich | 41¢ | | Hot Fudge Roast Beef Sandwich | 86¢ |
| Lemonade | + 23¢ | | Potato Chips | + 11¢ |
| total: | 64¢ | | total: | 97¢ |
| French Fries | 28¢ | | Ham & Jam Sandwich | 75¢ |
| Milk | + 31¢ | | Lemonade | + 23¢ |
| total: | 59¢ | | total: | 98¢ |
| Ham & Jam Sandwich | 75¢ | | Onion Rings | 37¢ |
| Potato Chips | + 11¢ | | Milk | + 31¢ |
| total: | 86¢ | | total: | 68¢ |
| Peanut Butter & Tuna Sandwich | 64¢ | | Lemonade | 23¢ |
| Lemonade | + 23¢ | | Milk | + 31¢ |
| total: | 87¢ | | total: | 54¢ |
| French Fries | 28¢ | | Onion Rings | 37¢ |
| Potato Chips | + 11¢ | | Raisin & Relish Sandwich | + 41¢ |
| total: | 39¢ | | total: | 78¢ |

Name _____

# Secret Sandwich

Solve the problems.
Match the letters to the numbered lines
  below to solve the riddle.

What is the
best-selling sandwich
at the Silly Sandwich Shop?

| 36¢<br>+ 45¢<br><br>= D | 57¢<br>+ 28¢<br><br>= P | 15¢<br>+ 26¢<br><br>= A | 72¢<br>+ 19¢<br><br>= M | 48¢<br>+ 39¢<br><br>= N | 54¢<br>+ 18¢<br><br>= T |
|---|---|---|---|---|---|
| 54¢<br>+ 38¢<br><br>= E | 25¢<br>+ 17¢<br><br>= R | 16¢<br>+ 77¢<br><br>= U | 37¢<br>+ 47¢<br><br>= B | 56¢<br>+ 18¢<br><br>= T | 49¢<br>+ 49¢<br><br>= U |
| 39¢<br>+ 11¢<br><br>= T | 76¢<br>+ 14¢<br><br>= U | 51¢<br>+ 19¢<br><br>= A | 22¢<br>+ 29¢<br><br>= T | 13¢<br>+ 18¢<br><br>= S | 31¢<br>+ 29¢<br><br>= E |

___  ___  ___  ___  ___  ___        ___  ___  ___  ___  ___  ___   and
85¢  60¢  70¢  87¢  90¢  72¢        84¢  93¢  51¢  74¢  92¢  42¢

___  ___  ___  ___  ___  ___  ___
91¢  98¢  31¢  50¢  41¢  42¢  81¢

**Bonus Box:** Invent your own silly sandwich. Write the ingredients on the back of this page.
Draw a picture of your silly sandwich and show it to a friend.

**Award**

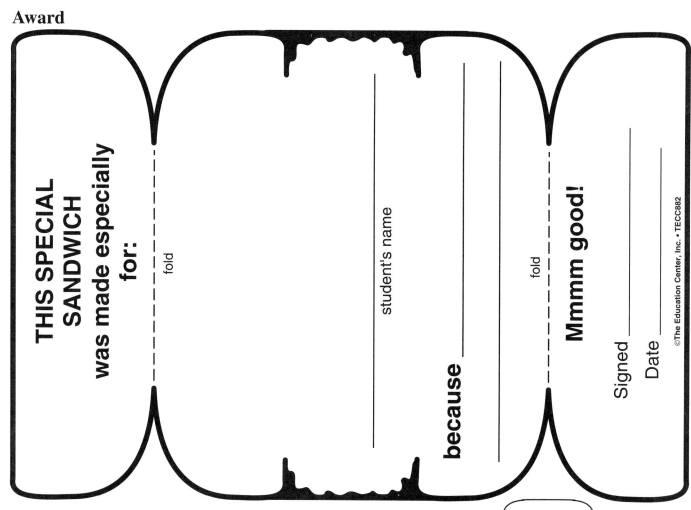

THIS SPECIAL
SANDWICH
was made especially
for:

fold

student's name

because

fold

Mmmm good!

Signed _____

Date _____

©The Education Center, Inc. • TECC882

**Note To Teacher:** Duplicate a copy of the sandwich award on construction paper for each of your students. Program the desired information; then fold forward on each award's dotted lines as shown and present the awards to your students.

Danny Overend
Student's name

## Answer Key

| 36¢<br>+ 45¢<br>81¢<br><br>= D | 57¢<br>+ 28¢<br>85¢<br><br>= P | 15¢<br>+ 26¢<br>41¢<br><br>= A | 72¢<br>+ 19¢<br>91¢<br><br>= M | 48¢<br>+ 39¢<br>87¢<br><br>= N | 54¢<br>+ 18¢<br>72¢<br><br>= T |
|---|---|---|---|---|---|
| 54¢<br>+ 38¢<br>92¢<br><br>= E | 25¢<br>+ 17¢<br>42¢<br><br>= R | 16¢<br>+ 77¢<br>93¢<br><br>= U | 37¢<br>+ 47¢<br>84¢<br><br>= B | 56¢<br>+ 18¢<br>74¢<br><br>= T | 49¢<br>+ 49¢<br>98¢<br><br>= U |
| 39¢<br>+ 11¢<br>50¢<br><br>= T | 76¢<br>+ 14¢<br>90¢<br><br>= U | 51¢<br>+ 19¢<br>70¢<br><br>= A | 22¢<br>+ 29¢<br>51¢<br><br>= T | 13¢<br>+ 18¢<br>31¢<br><br>= S | 31¢<br>+ 29¢<br>60¢<br><br>= E |

P     E     A     N     U     T              B     U     T     T     E     R     and
85¢  60¢  70¢  87¢  90¢  72¢          84¢  93¢  51¢  74¢  92¢  42¢

M     U     S     T     A     R     D
91¢  98¢  31¢  50¢  41¢  42¢  81¢

22

Subtraction: 2-digit, no regrouping

# Subtraction Sodas

Write the two numerals as a subtraction problem.
Solve each problem.

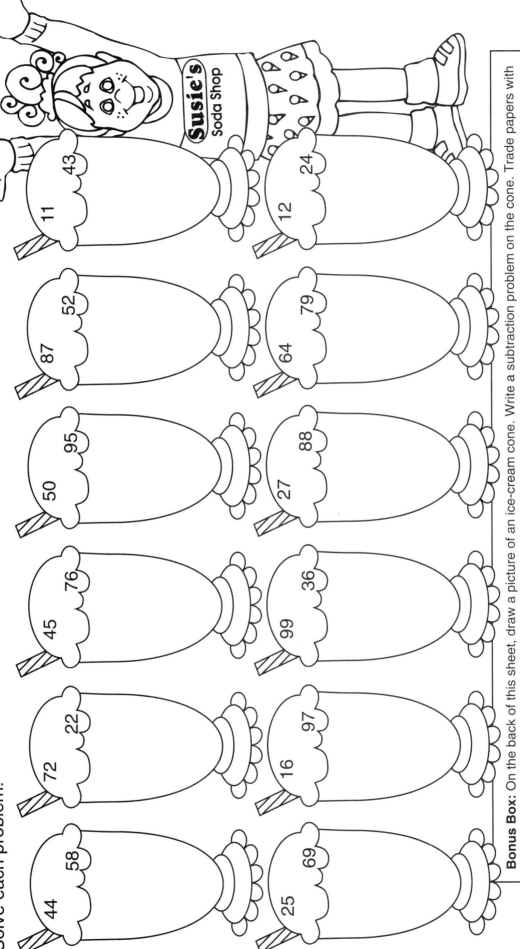

| 44 58 | 72 22 | 45 76 | 50 95 | 87 52 | 11 43 |
| 25 69 | 16 97 | 99 36 | 27 88 | 64 79 | 12 24 |

**Bonus Box:** On the back of this sheet, draw a picture of an ice-cream cone. Write a subtraction problem on the cone. Trade papers with a friend. Solve each other's problems.

©The Education Center, Inc. • TEC882

# Background For The Teacher
## Ice Cream

The main ingredients in ice cream are milk, cream, eggs, sugar, vanilla, and a small amount of salt. To make ice cream, the milk and cream are heated together. The eggs and sugar are added next. This mixture is heated to an extremely high temperature to kill germs. The mixture is then put into a machine called a *homogenizer*. This machine makes the ice cream smooth. Salt is added next, and then the mixture is cooled. After the mixture has cooled for a while, vanilla or other flavorings are added. Then the mixture is cooled down for several hours. Finally the mixture is cooled even more and then is quickly frozen. After the final freezing, the mixture has become ice cream. Other ingredients such as nuts, candy, and fruit can be added at this time.

How would you like to have a job as a professional ice-cream tester? When judging ice cream, professional ice-cream testers check for many things. They check to see if the color looks nice and if the color matches the flavor. They also check to see how quickly the ice cream melts. Professionals say that the best ice cream melts quickly at room temperature. Ice-cream testers look for ice cream that drips easily and feels smooth and creamy in the mouth.

# Follow-Up Activity
## Easy Ice Cream

Your class will love this tasty version of homemade ice cream. It's easy to make and you won't even need to use an ice-cream maker! To make a small batch of ice cream, you need the following ingredients:

    1 cup sugar
    1/2 cup milk
    1/2 cup cream
    1 tablespoon vanilla

Combine the ingredients in a bowl and let the mixture stand for a few minutes. Place the mixture in the freezer until it is partially frozen (approximately five hours). Remove the bowl from the freezer and beat the mixture until it is stiff. Freeze the mixture overnight. For a class of 30 students, this recipe makes enough ice cream for each child to have a spoonful.

## Answer Key

| 58 | 72 | 76 | 95 | 87 | 43 |
|----|----|----|----|----|----|
| − 44 | − 22 | − 45 | − 50 | − 52 | − 11 |
| 14 | 50 | 31 | 45 | 35 | 32 |

| 69 | 97 | 99 | 88 | 79 | 24 |
|----|----|----|----|----|----|
| − 25 | − 16 | − 36 | − 27 | − 64 | − 12 |
| 44 | 81 | 63 | 61 | 15 | 12 |

Name _____

# Susie's Soda Shop

Solve the problems.
Match the letters to the numbered lines below to solve the riddle.

Why are banana splits so attractive?

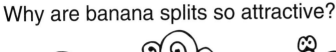

**Susie's**

| Popsicle | ..........25¢ |
| Cone | ..............75¢ |
| Shake | ............95¢ |
| Soda | ...............80¢ |
| Malt | .................95¢ |
| Banana Split | ..$3.00 |

| | | | | |
|---|---|---|---|---|
| 63<br>− 18<br><br>= O | 75<br>− 59<br><br>= N | 54<br>− 29<br><br>= L | 43<br>− 24<br><br>= T | 32<br>− 14<br><br>= H |
| 87<br>− 38<br><br>= P | 50<br>− 28<br><br>= F | 65<br>− 36<br><br>= E | 95<br>− 17<br><br>= E | 72<br>− 46<br><br>= V |
| 64<br>− 47<br><br>= Y | 46<br>− 19<br><br>= A | 71<br>− 59<br><br>= L | 90<br>− 53<br><br>= P | 85<br>− 38<br><br>= E |

___ ___ ___ ___   ___ ___ ___ ___
19  18  29  17    18  27  26  78

                    " ___ - ___ ___ ___ ___ "!
___ ___ ___ ___ ___ ___   ___ ___      ___   ___ ___ ___ ___
37  25  47  16  19  17    45  22      27    49  78  29  12

**Bonus Box:** On the back of this sheet, color a picture of a delicious ice-cream sundae. Below the picture, write about your sundae.

**Answer Key**

| | | | | |
|---|---|---|---|---|
| 63<br>− 18<br>45<br><br>= O | 75<br>− 59<br>16<br><br>= N | 54<br>− 29<br>25<br><br>= L | 43<br>− 24<br>19<br><br>= T | 32<br>− 14<br>18<br><br>= H |
| 87<br>− 38<br>49<br><br>= P | 50<br>− 28<br>22<br><br>= F | 65<br>− 36<br>29<br><br>= E | 95<br>− 17<br>78<br><br>= E | 72<br>− 46<br>26<br><br>= V |
| 64<br>− 47<br>17<br><br>= Y | 46<br>− 19<br>27<br><br>= A | 71<br>− 59<br>12<br><br>= L | 90<br>− 53<br>37<br><br>= P | 85<br>− 38<br>47<br><br>= E |

T   H   E   Y     H   A   V   E
19  18  29  17    18  27  26  78

P   L   E   N   T   Y     O   F   " A -  P   E   E   L "!
37  25  47  16  19  17    45  22    27   49  78  29  12

26

# Sweet Subtraction

Solve each problem.

An ice-cream sandwich costs 40¢. An ice-cream bar costs 45¢. How much more does an ice-cream bar cost than an ice-cream sandwich?

Three scoops on a cone cost 97¢. Two scoops cost 75¢. How much more do three scoops cost than two scoops?

Jim had 58¢. He bought an ice-cream bar for 45¢. How much money did he have left?

Two scoops on a cone cost 75¢. One scoop costs 50¢. How much more do two scoops cost than one scoop?

Jason has 21¢. A malt costs 95¢. How much more money does Jason need to buy a malt?

Emily had 85¢. She bought a Popsicle for 25¢. How much money did she have left?

A root-beer float costs 97¢. Patty has 35¢. How much more money does Patty need to buy a root-beer float?

A soda costs 83¢. A milkshake costs 99¢. How much more does a milkshake cost than a soda?

Whipped cream on a sundae costs 30¢. Nuts cost 55¢. How much more do nuts cost than whipped cream?

Susie's Soda Shop

A banana split costs 96¢. A sundae costs 62¢. How much more does a banana split cost than a sundae?

**Answer Key**

Name _____

Subtracting money word problems:
2-digit, no regrouping

# Sweet Subtraction

Solve each problem.

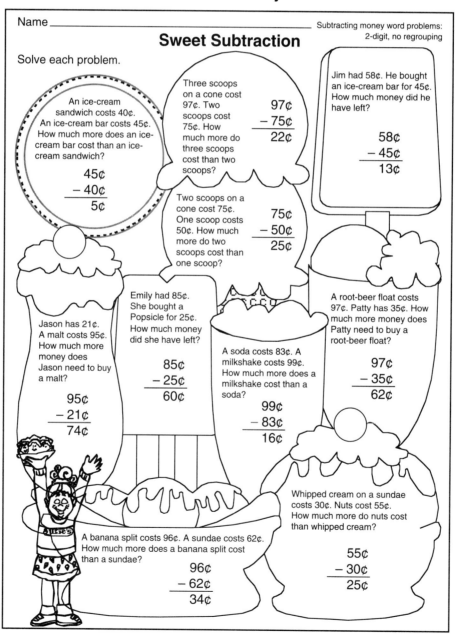

An ice-cream sandwich costs 40¢. An ice-cream bar costs 45¢. How much more does an ice-cream bar cost than an ice-cream sandwich?

$$45¢ - 40¢ = 5¢$$

Three scoops on a cone cost 97¢. Two scoops cost 75¢. How much more do three scoops cost than two scoops?

$$97¢ - 75¢ = 22¢$$

Jim had 58¢. He bought an ice-cream bar for 45¢. How much money did he have left?

$$58¢ - 45¢ = 13¢$$

Two scoops on a cone cost 75¢. One scoop costs 50¢. How much more do two scoops cost than one scoop?

$$75¢ - 50¢ = 25¢$$

Jason has 21¢. A malt costs 95¢. How much more money does Jason need to buy a malt?

$$95¢ - 21¢ = 74¢$$

Emily had 85¢. She bought a Popsicle for 25¢. How much money did she have left?

$$85¢ - 25¢ = 60¢$$

A root-beer float costs 97¢. Patty has 35¢. How much more money does Patty need to buy a root-beer float?

$$97¢ - 35¢ = 62¢$$

A soda costs 83¢. A milkshake costs 99¢. How much more does a milkshake cost than a soda?

$$99¢ - 83¢ = 16¢$$

A banana split costs 96¢. A sundae costs 62¢. How much more does a banana split cost than a sundae?

$$96¢ - 62¢ = 34¢$$

Whipped cream on a sundae costs 30¢. Nuts cost 55¢. How much more do nuts cost than whipped cream?

$$55¢ - 30¢ = 25¢$$

Name _____

# Warming Up!

Hank needs to check his work before he can work out.
Work each problem.
If Hank's answer is **correct**, draw a ★ beside it.
If Hank's answer is **incorrect**, draw a ✔ beside it.

1.  75
  − 23

2.  97
  − 86

3.  48
  − 12

4.  61
  − 10

5.  84
  − 32

6.  26
  − 14

7.  73
  − 41

8.  95
  − 24

9.  59
  − 37

10.  76
   − 12

11.  89
   − 33

12.  93
   − 50

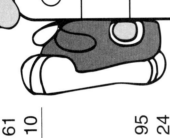

Hank

1. 52 ★        7. 52

2. 21          8. 71

3. 36          9. 23

4. 51          10. 64

5. 62          11. 56

6. 12          12. 33

**Bonus Box:** Add the answers from problems three and ten to find out how much a baby hippo weighs.

## How To Use The Pencil Topper Below

Duplicate student copies of the pencil topper below. Have students color and cut out their toppers. Assist students in carefully cutting along the dotted lines to make slits. Students place their pencil toppers on their pencils to help warm up for subtraction!

## Pencil-Topper Pattern

©The Education Center, Inc.

Cut on dotted line.

## Answer Key

| Actual Answers To Problems | Answers On Hank's Paper |
|---|---|
| 1. 52 | 1. 52 ★ |
| 2. 11 | 2. 21 ✔ |
| 3. 36 | 3. 36 ★ |
| 4. 51 | 4. 51 ★ |
| 5. 52 | 5. 62 ✔ |
| 6. 12 | 6. 12 ★ |
| 7. 32 | 7. 52 ✔ |
| 8. 71 | 8. 71 ★ |
| 9. 22 | 9. 23 ✔ |
| 10. 64 | 10. 64 ★ |
| 11. 56 | 11. 56 ★ |
| 12. 43 | 12. 33 ✔ |

**Bonus Box Answer**
A baby hippo weighs about 100 pounds at birth.

Problems:
1. 95 - 17
2. 63 - 57
3. 84 - 18
4. 86 - 69
5. 75 - 29
6. 91 - 68
7. 97 - 28
8. 54 - 28
9. 81 - 23
10. 52 - 38
11. 61 - 12
12. 72 - 35

Locker numbers: 26, 66, 14, 78, 49, 17, 46, 58, 23, 6, 69, 37

# Exercise Is For Hippos!

Solve each problem.
Show your work.
Cross out the answers on the locker to check.

| 26 | | 14 |
|----|----|----|
| | 66 | |
| 78 | | 17 |
| 46 | 49 | |
| | | 58 |
| 23 | 6 | |
| | | 69 |
| | 37 | |

1.  95
   − 17

2.  63
   − 57

3.  84
   − 18

4.  86
   − 69

5.  75
   − 29

6.  91
   − 68

7.  97
   − 28

8.  54
   − 28

9.  81
   − 23

10.  52
    − 38

11.  61
    − 12

12.  72
    − 35

**Bonus Box:** On another sheet of paper, write a story about a hippo. Make up your own title or use one of the following: *The Day A Hippo Followed Me To School, How To Hide A Hippo,* or *Harold The Horrible Hippo.*

## Extension Activity
## Hippo Break!

Use the hippo pattern below to give your children Hippo Breaks for addition practice. Duplicate the pattern for each child. Then have each child cut out her hippo and store it in a safe place in her desk. Periodically, call out "Hippo Break!" Students take out their hippo patterns and listen carefully as you dictate five addition problems. Each child writes the problems on her hippo pattern and then quickly solves them. Check the answers as a group. Students eagerly await their next Hippo Break.

## Pattern

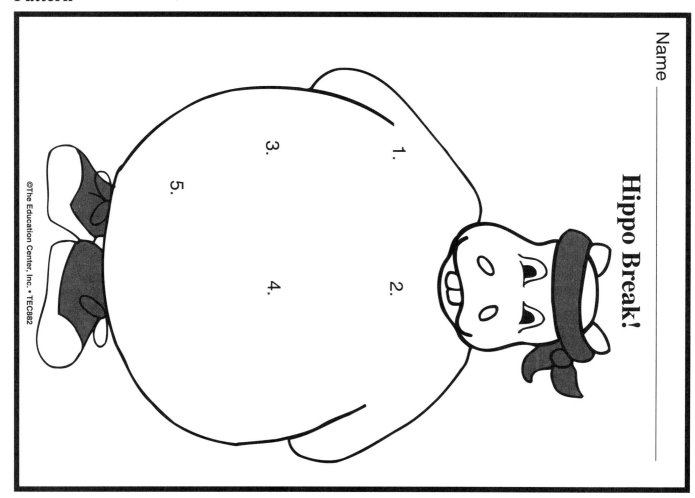

©The Education Center, Inc. • TEC882

Name

Hippo Break!

**Answer Key**

1. 78
2. 6
3. 66
4. 17
5. 46
6. 23
7. 69
8. 26
9. 58
10. 14
11. 49
12. 37

# Hip, Hip, "Hippo-ray"!

Solve the problems.
Match the letters to the numbered lines below to solve the riddle.
The first one has been done for you.

**What kind of exercise does a hippo do?**

| | | | |
|---|---|---|---|
| 814<br>− 703<br>**111**<br><br>= O | 673<br>− 541<br><br><br>= H | 935<br>− 821<br><br><br>= P | 584<br>− 102<br><br><br>= R |
| 456<br>− 316<br><br><br>= C | 345<br>− 132<br><br><br>= ! | 674<br>− 142<br><br><br>= I | 887<br>− 706<br><br><br>= B |
| 313<br>− 210<br><br><br>= P | 499<br>− 227<br><br><br>= I | 780<br>− 430<br><br><br>= O | 984<br>− 372<br><br><br>= S |

___ ___ ___ ___ ___  -  ___ ___  ⃝  ___ ___ ___ ___ ___
132  272  103  114  350     482  111    181  532  140  612  213

You can work out too!

1. Stretch up high
   and count to five.

2. Touch the floor
   and count to five.

3. Put your hands on your
   hips and turn from left to
   right five times.

## How To Use This Award

Duplicate student copies of the hippo award. Cut out each award and fold on the dotted lines as shown in the illustration. Personalize each award before presenting it to a student.

**Award**

Sample Award

### Answer Key

| | | | |
|---|---|---|---|
| 814<br>− 703<br>**111** | 673<br>− 541<br>**132** | 935<br>− 821<br>114 | 584<br>− 102<br>**482** |
| = O | = H | = P | = R |
| 456<br>− 316<br>**140** | 345<br>− 132<br>**213** | 674<br>− 142<br>**532** | 887<br>− 706<br>**181** |
| = C | = ! | = I | = B |
| 313<br>− 210<br>**103** | 499<br>− 227<br>**272** | 780<br>− 430<br>**350** | 984<br>− 372<br>**612** |
| = P | = I | = O | = S |

H I P P O - R O B I C S !
132 272 103 114 350   482 111 181 532 140 612 213

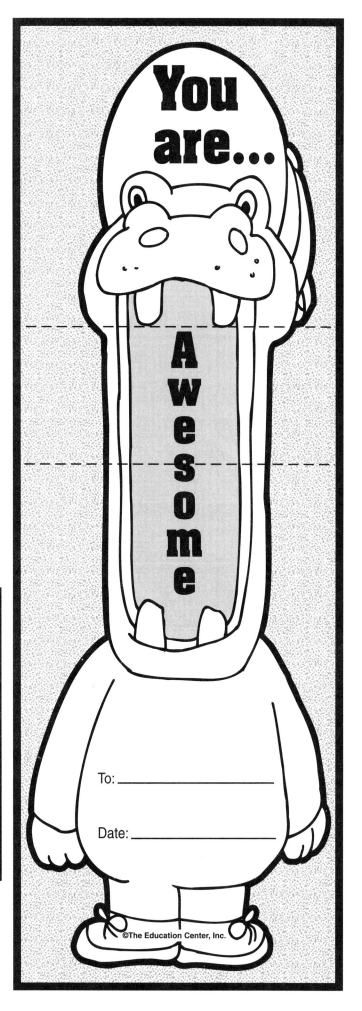

©The Education Center, Inc.

34

Name _____

# In Tip-top Shape

Solve each problem.
Check your work with addition.
The first one has been done for you.

1.
```
   8 1
   94        →    69
 − 25          + 25
 ─────         ─────
   69             94
```

2.
```
   81
 − 29        +
 ─────       ─────
```

3.
```
   62
 − 33        +
 ─────       ─────
```

4.
```
   53
 − 18        +
 ─────       ─────
```

5.
```
   74
 − 57        +
 ─────       ─────
```

6.
```
   63
 − 29        +
 ─────       ─────
```

7.
```
   52
 − 37        +
 ─────       ─────
```

8.
```
   86
 − 49        +
 ─────       ─────
```

9.
```
   45
 − 17        +
 ─────       ─────
```

10.
```
   54
 − 27        +
 ─────       ─────
```

11.
```
   62
 − 19        +
 ─────       ─────
```

12.
```
   93
 − 55        +
 ─────       ─────
```

**Bonus Box:** On the back of this sheet, draw and color a picture of yourself doing your favorite exercise. Write a sentence telling about your picture.

## Answer Key

| | | | | | | | |
|---|---|---|---|---|---|---|---|
| 1. | $^{8}$ $^{1}$ 94 → 69 | 69 | 2. | $^{7}$ $_{1}$ 81 | 52 | 3. | $^{5}$ $_{1}$ 62 | 29 |

1.  
   $^{8}$ $^{1}$  
   94 → 69  
 − 25    + 25  
  69     94

2.  
  $^{7}$ $_{1}$  
  81     52  
 − 29    + 29  
  52     81

3.  
  $^{5}$ $_{1}$  
  62     29  
 − 33    + 33  
  29     62

4.  
  $^{4}$ $_{1}$  
  53     35  
 − 18    + 18  
  35     53

5.  
  $^{6}$ $_{1}$  
  74     17  
 − 57    + 57  
  17     74

6.  
  $^{5}$ $_{1}$  
  63     34  
 − 29    + 29  
  34     63

7.  
  $^{4}$ $_{1}$  
  52     15  
 − 37    + 37  
  15     52

8.  
  $^{7}$ $_{1}$  
  86     37  
 − 49    + 49  
  37     86

9.  
  $^{3}$ $_{1}$  
  45     28  
 − 17    + 17  
  28     45

10.  
  $^{4}$ $_{1}$  
  54     27  
 − 27    + 27  
  27     54

11.  
  $^{5}$ $_{1}$  
  62     43  
 − 19    + 19  
  43     62

12.  
  $^{8}$ $_{1}$  
  93     38  
 − 55    + 55  
  38     93

Name _____

# Doing The Turtle Tango

Solve the problems.
Cut out and glue an answer to each turtle.

12
− 6

8
+ 8

14
− 7

9
+ 9

16
− 8

7
+ 7

8
+ 9

13
− 8

7
+ 8

6
+ 6

13
− 9

18
− 9

©The Education Center, Inc. • TEC882

18    4    14    9    17    7

6    16    5    15    8    12

**Bonus Box:** Design a new type of hat for these turtles. Draw it on the back.

## Extension Activity
## Turtle Tie!

Your students will be eager to practice their addition facts as they play this fun game! For each pair of students, duplicate 20 of the turtle cards below on green construction paper. Cut out the cards and label each one with a desired one-digit number. To play, students divide the cards between them and stack the cards facedown. Simultaneously, students turn over the top cards to reveal the numbers. The first student to add the numbers together and tell the correct sum gets to place both cards at the bottom of his stack. If the two cards revealed have the same number, the first child to say "Turtle Tie" wins the cards. Play continues in this manner until one player has all of the cards in his stack.

## Turtle Cards

©The Education Center, Inc.   ©The Education Center, Inc.   ©The Education Center, Inc.   ©The Education Center, Inc.

## Answer Key

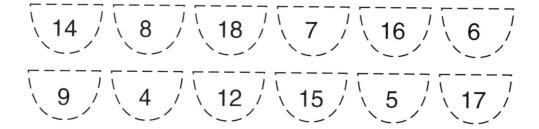

14    8    18    7    16    6

9    4    12    15    5    17

Name _____

## Totally Turtle

**Example:**

Solve the problems.
Color and cut out the pieces.
Glue the turtle together as shown.

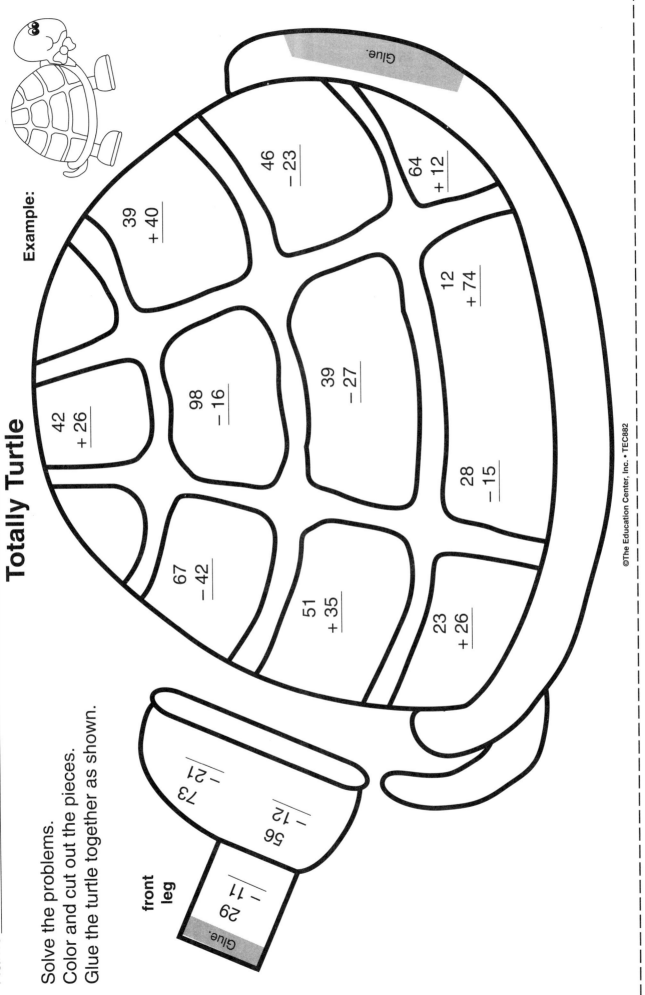

front
leg

$$\begin{array}{r} 42 \\ +\,26 \\ \hline \end{array}$$

$$\begin{array}{r} 39 \\ +\,40 \\ \hline \end{array}$$

$$\begin{array}{r} 46 \\ -\,23 \\ \hline \end{array}$$

$$\begin{array}{r} 64 \\ +\,12 \\ \hline \end{array}$$

$$\begin{array}{r} 98 \\ -\,16 \\ \hline \end{array}$$

$$\begin{array}{r} 39 \\ -\,27 \\ \hline \end{array}$$

$$\begin{array}{r} 12 \\ +\,74 \\ \hline \end{array}$$

$$\begin{array}{r} 67 \\ -\,42 \\ \hline \end{array}$$

$$\begin{array}{r} 51 \\ +\,35 \\ \hline \end{array}$$

$$\begin{array}{r} 28 \\ -\,15 \\ \hline \end{array}$$

$$\begin{array}{r} 23 \\ +\,26 \\ \hline \end{array}$$

$$\begin{array}{r} 73 \\ -\,21 \\ \hline \end{array}$$

$$\begin{array}{r} 56 \\ -\,12 \\ \hline \end{array}$$

$$\begin{array}{r} 29 \\ -\,11 \\ \hline \end{array}$$

Glue.

Glue.

Glue.

**Note To Teacher:** Use this page with page 40.

## How To Use Pages 39 And 40

Duplicate student copies of pages 39 and 40. Cut on the dotted line on page 40 before passing the sheets out.

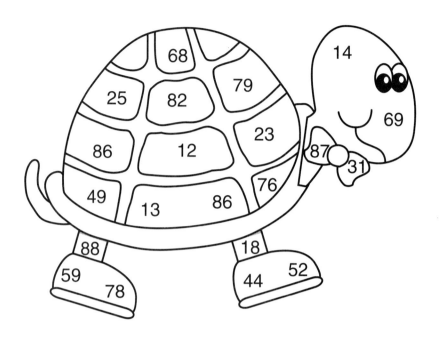

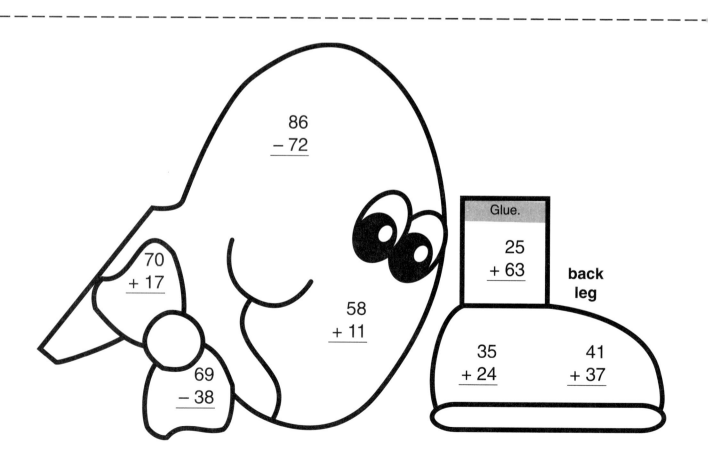

# Let's Talk Turtle

Solve the problems.
To solve the riddle, match the letters to the
  numbered lines below.

What do turtles wear
to keep warm?

| 72 <br> + 19 <br><br> = C | 63 <br> − 57 <br><br> = N | 56 <br> + 18 <br><br> = P | 86 <br> − 69 <br><br> = E | 15 <br> + 26 <br><br> = A | 97 <br> − 28 <br><br> = P |
|---|---|---|---|---|---|
| 13 <br> + 18 <br><br> = E | 91 <br> − 68 <br><br> = L | 25 <br> + 17 <br><br> = R | 52 <br> − 38 <br><br> = E | 47 <br> + 39 <br><br> = T | 72 <br> − 35 <br><br> = S |
| 11 <br> + 39 <br><br> = K | 47 <br> − 38 <br><br> = E | 36 <br> + 45 <br><br> = O | 55 <br> − 17 <br><br> = S | 16 <br> + 77 <br><br> = E | 80 <br> − 35 <br><br> = W |

 74  14  81  69  23  31  6  17  91  50    38  45  9  41  86  93  42  37

## Answer Key

| | | | | | |
|---|---|---|---|---|---|
| 72<br>+ 19<br>91<br><br>= C | 63<br>− 57<br>6<br><br>= N | 56<br>+ 18<br>74<br><br>= P | 86<br>− 69<br>17<br><br>= E | 15<br>+ 26<br>41<br><br>= A | 97<br>− 28<br>69<br><br>= P |
| 13<br>+ 18<br>31<br><br>= E | 91<br>− 68<br>23<br><br>= L | 25<br>+ 17<br>42<br><br>= R | 52<br>− 38<br>14<br><br>= E | 47<br>+ 39<br>86<br><br>= T | 72<br>− 35<br>37<br><br>= S |
| 11<br>+ 39<br>50<br><br>= K | 47<br>− 38<br>9<br><br>= E | 36<br>+ 45<br>81<br><br>= O | 55<br>− 17<br>38<br><br>= S | 16<br>+ 77<br>93<br><br>= E | 80<br>− 35<br>45<br><br>= W |

**Answer To Riddle:**

P E O P L E N E C K     S W E A T E R S
74 14 81 69 23 31 6 17 91 50     38 45 9 41 86 93 42 37

42

Name _____

# Tic-Tac-Turtle

1. In turn, work a problem.
2. Color the egg; then write your name in the box.
3. Try to get three in a row.

## Game 1

| 37<br>+ 27 | 43<br>− 29 | 45<br>+ 18 |
|---|---|---|
| 86<br>− 49 | 18<br>+ 12 | 72<br>− 37 |
| 78<br>+ 16 | 43<br>− 27 | 36<br>+ 46 |

Eggs: 14 30 63 94 37 35 64 82 16

## Game 2

| 88<br>− 39 | 33<br>+ 39 | 95<br>− 17 |
|---|---|---|
| 39<br>+ 18 | 50<br>− 28 | 38<br>+ 26 |
| 85<br>− 59 | 67<br>+ 25 | 53<br>− 19 |

Eggs: 49 92 34 78 26 64 72 57 22

43

# How To Use Page 43

Your students will have a terrific time playing Tic-Tac-Turtle. Duplicate one copy of page 43 for every two students. Have the children play Tic-Tac-Turtle in pairs. Before beginning, have each twosome cut its game sheet in half and set Game 2 aside. To begin play, each child flips a coin to see who will be X and O. The X player begins Game 1 by choosing a problem to solve. Then he writes the answer under the problem, colors the turtle egg with that answer, and puts an X in the box. Next the O player chooses a problem and repeats the same process. Each twosome continues to alternate play until one person scores tic-tac-turtle or until all of the squares have been marked. The children may play another game of Tic-Tac-Turtle by using Game 2. The O player begins Game 2.

**Answer Key**

| 64 | 14 | 63 |
|----|----|----|
| 37 | 30 | 35 |
| 94 | 16 | 82 |

| 49 | 72 | 78 |
|----|----|----|
| 57 | 22 | 64 |
| 26 | 92 | 34 |

Name _____

# Field Trip To The Zoo

Solve each problem.
Show your work in the space below each problem.

1. The painted turtle exhibit has 11 small turtles and 15 large turtles. How many turtles are there altogether?

2. One side-necked turtle laid 12 eggs. Another laid 13 eggs. How many eggs were there altogether?

3. The snapping turtle's cage is 24 inches long. The snapping turtle is 8 inches long. How much longer is the cage than the turtle?

4. The box turtle walked 27 inches. Then he walked 13 more inches. How far did he walk?

5. The desert tortoise had 16 tasty leaves. He ate 12. How many leaves were left?

6. There are 22 children in a class. 11 children visited the green turtle exhibit. How many children did not visit this exhibit?

7. The soft-shelled turtles ate 19 insects and 17 snails. How many creatures did they eat altogether?

## How To Use This Award

Duplicate copies of the award badge below on green construction paper. Cut out each turtle and turtle shell. To assemble each badge, attach the shell to the turtle by inserting a small brad through the Xs. When a child successfully completes a desired math goal, pin a personalized badge to his shirt. The child can then slide the shell away from the turtle to reveal a special message.

## Turtle-Badge Patterns

**Example:**

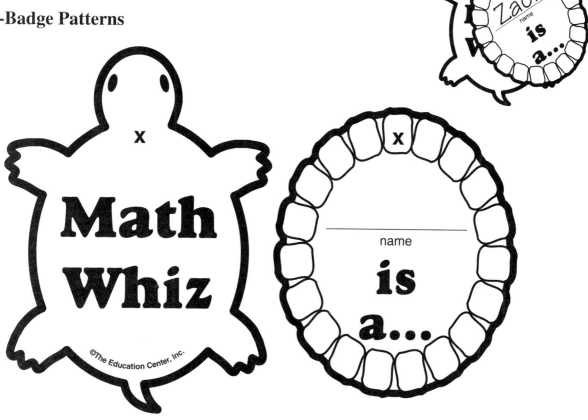

©The Education Center, Inc.

### Answer Key

1.  $\begin{array}{r} 11 \\ + 15 \\ \hline 26 \end{array}$ turtles

2.  $\begin{array}{r} 12 \\ + 13 \\ \hline 25 \end{array}$ eggs

3.  $\begin{array}{r} 24 \\ - 8 \\ \hline 16 \end{array}$ inches

4.  $\begin{array}{r} 27 \\ + 13 \\ \hline 40 \end{array}$ inches

5.  $\begin{array}{r} 16 \\ - 12 \\ \hline 4 \end{array}$ leaves

6.  $\begin{array}{r} 22 \\ - 11 \\ \hline 11 \end{array}$ children

7.  $\begin{array}{r} 19 \\ + 17 \\ \hline 36 \end{array}$ creatures

# Grinning Giraffes

Solve the facts.

| 5 | 2 | 7 | 8 | 1 |
|---|---|---|---|---|
| + 8 | + 9 | + 7 | + 6 | + 4 |

7 + 5 = _____     4 + 4 = _____     9 + 4 = _____

5 + 6 = _____     8 + 8 = _____     5 + 9 = _____

8 + 9 = _____     3 + 8 = _____     7 + 9 = _____

6 + 7 = _____     9 + 9 = _____     6 + 3 = _____

2 + 5 = _____     4 + 7 = _____     8 + 3 = _____

How to Spot A Giraffe

**Bonus Box:**
Draw an orange circle around each sum that is greater than 10. You should have 18 circles.

| 7 | 4 | 8 | 9 | 3 |
|---|---|---|---|---|
| + 8 | + 5 | + 2 | + 6 | + 7 |

©The Education Center, Inc. • TEC882

1

---

# Where Is That Lion?

Solve the facts.

18 − 9 = _____     13 − 6 = _____     12 − 9 = _____     14 − 6 = _____

14 − 9 = _____     13 − 5 = _____     11 − 4 = _____

| 16 | 15 | 10 | 16 | 14 | 11 |
|---|---|---|---|---|---|
| − 8 | − 9 | − 6 | − 9 | − 5 | − 7 |

| 17 | 11 | 16 | 12 | 13 |
|---|---|---|---|---|
| − 8 | − 2 | − 7 | − 7 | − 8 |

13 − 4 = _____     15 − 7 = _____

12 − 5 = _____     13 − 7 = _____

**Bonus Box:**
If you have six facts that equal nine, color the lion's nose pink.

©The Education Center, Inc. • TEC882

2

47

## How To Use This Unit

— This math review unit is designed to be a booklet when completed. The booklet consists of eight individual math activities and a student-made cover (page 50). If desired, have students complete the cover first, then complete each booklet page on a different day. (Finished booklet pages can be stored inside the completed cover until all pages are done.)

— To make the **booklet cover**, have each student personalize, color, and cut out a copy of the cover pattern on page 50. Next have the student fold a 9" x 12" sheet of green construction paper in half. Then, keeping the fold at the top, have the student glue his cutout atop the folded paper.

— To prepare the **booklet pages**, duplicate student copies of pages 47, 49, 51, and 53. Then cut apart each page to create a total of eight math activities. When your students have completed their final booklet page, have each student stack his pages in order. Then help each youngster staple his pages inside his booklet cover.

## Safari-Style Pencil Toppers

Students are certain to follow the call of the wild when they top their pencils with these adorable critters. Using the patterns on page 52, duplicate a desired number of pencil toppers onto white construction paper. Carefully slit on the dashed lines with an X-acto knife. For added fun, place the toppers in a safari-type hat and have each student draw a topper from the hat. Then have each youngster color and cut out his topper before carefully slipping it onto his pencil.

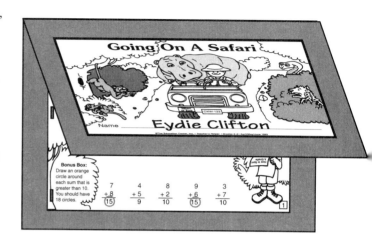

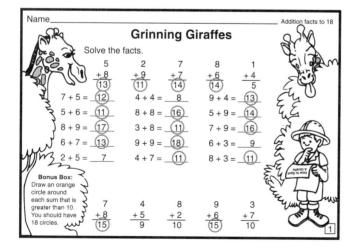

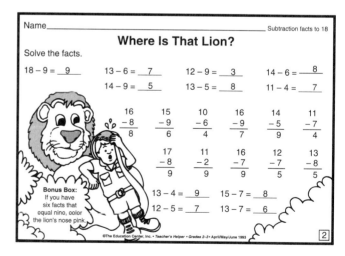

# Hide-And-Seek

Solve each fact.
Cross out a matching answer on the bush.

| 12 | 18 | 9 | 8 | 11 | 3 |
|---|---|---|---|---|---|
| − 8 | − 9 | + 5 | + 8 | − 6 | + 9 |

| 7 | 8 | 17 | 15 | 9 | 15 | 14 |
|---|---|---|---|---|---|---|
| + 6 | + 7 | − 9 | − 8 | + 7 | − 6 | − 8 |

```
        7
   13      16
    5      12
   15   17   9
   11        4
    6   16    8
   14    9    7
```

| 13 | 6 | 9 |
|---|---|---|
| − 6 | + 5 | + 8 |

peanuts

3

---

# Some Monkey Business

Solve the facts.

| 3 | 6 | 15 | 6 | 12 | 8 | 13 |
|---|---|---|---|---|---|---|
| + 8 | + 8 | − 7 | + 9 | − 6 | + 9 | − 5 |

| 8 | 14 | 9 | 8 | 13 | 16 |
|---|---|---|---|---|---|
| + 5 | − 7 | + 9 | + 4 | − 8 | − 7 |

| 9 | 12 | 16 | 13 | 7 |
|---|---|---|---|---|
| + 7 | − 3 | − 8 | − 9 | + 7 |

MONKEYS

**Bonus Box:** Draw a green circle around each even answer.
Draw a yellow square around each odd answer.

4

# Booklet Cover

Use with "How To Use This Unit" on page 48.

# Going On A Safari

Name _____

---

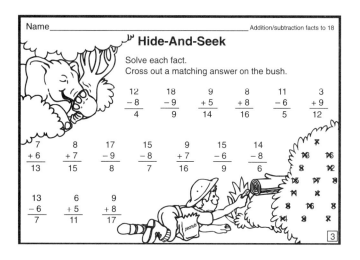

Name_____  Addition/subtraction facts to 18

## Hide-And-Seek

Solve each fact.
Cross out a matching answer on the bush.

| 12<br>− 8<br>4 | 18<br>− 9<br>9 | 9<br>+ 5<br>14 | 8<br>+ 8<br>16 | 11<br>− 6<br>5 | 3<br>+ 9<br>12 |
|---|---|---|---|---|---|

| 7<br>+ 6<br>13 | 8<br>+ 7<br>15 | 17<br>− 9<br>8 | 15<br>− 8<br>7 | 9<br>+ 7<br>16 | 15<br>− 6<br>9 | 14<br>− 8<br>6 |
|---|---|---|---|---|---|---|

| 13<br>− 6<br>7 | 6<br>+ 5<br>11 | 9<br>+ 8<br>17 |
|---|---|---|

3

---

Name_____  Addition/subtraction facts to 18

## Some Monkey Business

Solve the facts.

| 3<br>+ 8<br>[11] | 6<br>+ 8<br>(14) | 15<br>− 7<br>(8) | 6<br>+ 9<br>[15] | 12<br>− 6<br>(6) | 8<br>+ 9<br>[17] | 13<br>− 5<br>(8) |
|---|---|---|---|---|---|---|

| 8<br>+ 5<br>[13] | 14<br>− 7<br>[7] | 9<br>+ 9<br>(18) | 8<br>+ 4<br>[12] | 13<br>− 8<br>[5] | 16<br>− 7<br>[9] |
|---|---|---|---|---|---|

| 9<br>+ 7<br>(16) | 12<br>− 3<br>[9] | 16<br>− 8<br>(8) | 13<br>− 9<br>(4) | 7<br>+ 7<br>(14) |
|---|---|---|---|---|

**Bonus Box:** Draw a green circle around each even answer.
Draw a yellow square around each odd answer.

4

50

Addition/subtraction: no regrouping

# Spotting A Cheetah

Solve each problem.
Color the matching answer below.

| 45 | 42 | 29 | 94 | 39 | 58 |
|---|---|---|---|---|---|
| + 12 | + 26 | − 14 | − 61 | + 40 | − 23 |

| 63 | 35 | 76 | 63 | 25 |
|---|---|---|---|---|
| + 34 | − 24 | + 23 | − 32 | + 63 |

| 76 | 22 | 82 | 37 |
|---|---|---|---|
| − 34 | + 62 | − 11 | + 21 |

| 58 | 47 | 39 |
|---|---|---|
| + 21 | − 31 | − 15 |

Cheetah Chow

5

Addition: mixed practice

# Getting The Point!

Solve the problems.

| 42 | 58 | 51 | 47 | 19 |
|---|---|---|---|---|
| + 26 | + 26 | + 35 | + 72 | + 18 |

| 12 | 76 | 39 | 27 | 64 |
|---|---|---|---|---|
| + 74 | + 23 | + 24 | + 28 | + 35 |

| | 63 | 82 | 17 | 58 |
|---|---|---|---|---|
| | + 75 | + 13 | + 61 | + 34 |

| | 24 | 63 | 39 | 56 |
|---|---|---|---|---|
| | + 35 | + 36 | + 47 | + 83 |

**Bonus Box:** Draw a blue circle around each problem that required regrouping. You should have nine problems circled.

6

# Pencil Topper Patterns
Use with "Safari-Style Pencil Toppers" on page 48.

©TEC882

©TEC882

©TEC882

©TEC882

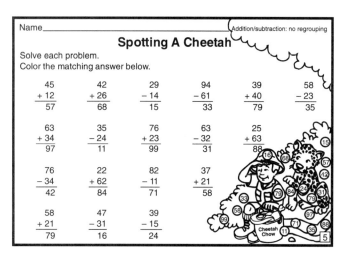

Name_____

## Spotting A Cheetah

Solve each problem.
Color the matching answer below.

| 45 + 12 = 57 | 42 + 26 = 68 | 29 − 14 = 15 | 94 − 61 = 33 | 39 + 40 = 79 | 58 − 23 = 35 |
|---|---|---|---|---|---|
| 63 + 34 = 97 | 35 − 24 = 11 | 76 + 23 = 99 | 63 − 32 = 31 | 25 + 63 = 88 | |
| 76 − 34 = 42 | 22 + 62 = 84 | 82 − 11 = 71 | 37 + 21 = 58 | | |
| 58 + 21 = 79 | 47 − 31 = 16 | 39 − 15 = 24 | | | |

Cheetah Chow

5

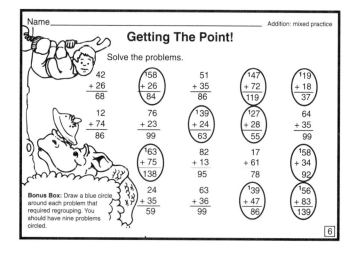

Name_____

## Getting The Point!

Solve the problems.

| 42 + 26 = 68 | 158 + 26 = 84 | 51 + 35 = 86 | 147 + 72 = 119 | 119 + 18 = 37 |
|---|---|---|---|---|
| 12 + 74 = 86 | 76 + 23 = 99 | 139 + 24 = 63 | 127 + 28 = 55 | 64 + 35 = 99 |
| | 163 + 75 = 138 | 82 + 13 = 95 | 17 + 61 = 78 | 158 + 34 = 92 |
| | 24 + 35 = 59 | 63 + 36 = 99 | 139 + 47 = 86 | 156 + 83 = 139 |

**Bonus Box:** Draw a blue circle around each problem that required regrouping. You should have nine problems circled.

6

52

# Hip, Hip, Hippopotamus!

Name_____

Solve the problems.

| | | | | |
|---|---|---|---|---|
| 64<br>− 29 | 77<br>− 23 | 82<br>− 28 | 90<br>− 63 | 68<br>−15 |
| 38<br>− 13 | 87<br>− 23 | 72<br>− 37 | 93<br>− 38 | 35<br>− 22 |
| | 85<br>− 27 | 66<br>− 49 | | |

**Bonus Box:** Draw a green lily pad around each answer that has five tens. You should draw five lily pads!

7

---

Name_____

# A Wild Ride

Solve the problems.

| | | | | |
|---|---|---|---|---|
| 67<br>− 45 | 84<br>− 16 | 39<br>+ 26 | 46<br>− 23 | 34<br>+ 17 |
| 24<br>+ 65 | 77<br>− 26 | 85<br>+ 33 | 36<br>− 29 | 65<br>+ 25 |
| 88<br>+ 71 | 64<br>+ 33 | 73<br>− 35 | 25<br>+ 37 | 45<br>− 26 |
| | 91<br>− 40 | 52<br>+ 29 | 74<br>− 37 | |

**Bonus Box:** Draw a red heart around the problem having the largest answer.

8

Subtraction: mixed practice

# Hip, Hip, Hippopotamus!

Solve the problems.

| | | | | |
|---|---|---|---|---|
| ⁵6̸4 − 29 = 35 | 77 − 23 = (54) | ⁷8̸2 − 28 = (54) | ⁸9̸0 − 63 = 27 | 68 − 15 = (53) |
| 38 − 13 = 25 | 87 − 23 = 64 | ⁶¹7̸2 − 37 = 35 | ⁸¹9̸3 − 38 = (55) | 35 − 22 = 13 |
| | ⁷¹8̸5 − 27 = (58) | ⁵¹6̸6 − 49 = 17 | | |

**Bonus Box:** Draw a green lily pad around each answer that has five tens. You should draw five lily pads!

7

Addition/subtraction: mixed practice

# A Wild Ride

Solve the problems.

| | | | | |
|---|---|---|---|---|
| 67 − 45 = 22 | ⁷¹8̸4 − 16 = 68 | ¹39 + 26 = 65 | 46 − 23 = 23 | ¹34 + 17 = 51 |
| 24 + 65 = 89 | 77 − 26 = 51 | ¹85 + 33 = 118 | ²¹8̸6 − 29 = 7 | ¹65 + 25 = 90 |
| ¹88 + 71 = 159 | 64 + 33 = 97 | ⁶¹7̸3 − 35 = 38 | ¹25 + 37 = 62 | ³¹4̸5 − 26 = 19 |
| | 91 − 40 = 51 | ¹52 + 29 = 81 | ⁶¹7̸4 − 37 = 37 | |

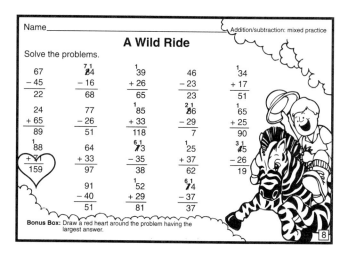

**Bonus Box:** Draw a red heart around the problem having the largest answer.

8

54

Name _____

# The Breakfast Stop

Read each problem carefully.
Solve each problem.
Show your work.
Fill in the circle.

1. Joe made 46 blueberry pancakes and 51 apple pancakes Monday morning. How many pancakes did Joe make altogether?
   ○ Joe made 95 pancakes.
   ○ Joe made 97 pancakes.
   ○ Not given.

2. On Tuesday, 64 cheese Danish and 25 apple Danish were served. How many Danish were served in all?
   ○ 89 Danish were served.
   ○ 39 Danish were served.
   ○ Not given.

3. Wednesday's morning special was scrambled eggs, bacon, and toast. 17 people ordered the special between 6:30 and 7:30. 32 people ordered it between 7:30 and 8:30. How many specials were ordered in all?
   ○ 15 specials were ordered.
   ○ 49 specials were ordered.
   ○ Not given.

4. 27 people ordered muffins and juice on Tuesday. On Wednesday, 42 people ordered muffins and juice. How many people ordered muffins and juice altogether?
   ○ 25 people ordered muffins and juice.
   ○ 68 people ordered muffins and juice.
   ○ Not given.

5. On Friday, 25 customers ordered 34 jelly-filled doughnuts and 63 glazed doughnuts. How many doughnuts were ordered in all?
   ○ 97 doughnuts were ordered.
   ○ 59 doughnuts were ordered.
   ○ Not given.

6. On Saturday, 36 people ordered scrambled eggs with ham. 22 people ordered pancakes with sausage. How many breakfasts were ordered altogether?
   ○ 14 breakfasts were ordered.
   ○ 68 breakfasts were ordered.
   ○ Not given.

7. Seth made 32 servings of French toast with syrup and 53 servings of French toast with powdered sugar on Sunday morning. How many servings of French toast did Seth make in all?
   ○ Seth made 75 servings of French toast.
   ○ Seth made 85 servings of French toast.
   ○ Not given.

8. On Thursday, Jean poured 52 cups of coffee from 7:30 to 8:30. From 8:30 to 9:30 she poured 33 cups of coffee. How many cups of coffee did Jean pour in all?
   ○ Jean poured 88 cups of coffee.
   ○ Jean poured 16 cups of coffee.
   ○ Not given.

**Bonus Box:** On the back of this sheet, draw and color a picture of yourself eating your favorite breakfast. Yum!

# Extension Activity
# Fast-Food Story Problems

Duplicate student copies of the food cards below. Have each child color and cut out the cards. Then have students work in pairs to write fast-food story problems using various items on the cards. Have each pair exchange story problems with another pair of students and then work together to solve the problems.

## Food Cards

| doughnut | salad | french fries | ice-cream cone |
| 15¢ | 68¢ | 47¢ | 50¢ |
| fried eggs | pizza | hot dog | pickle |
| 55¢ | 96¢ | 73¢ | 16¢ |
| pancakes | drink | hamburger | potato chips |
| 39¢ | 24¢ | 82¢ | 21¢ |

### Answer Key

1. Joe made 97 pancakes.
2. 89 Danish were served.
3. 49 specials were ordered.
4. Not given.
5. 97 doughnuts were ordered.
6. Not given.
7. Seth made 85 servings of French toast.
8. Not given.

Name _____

# Stop 'N' Go Munchies

Read each problem carefully.
Solve each problem on the order pad.
Use the menu to help you.

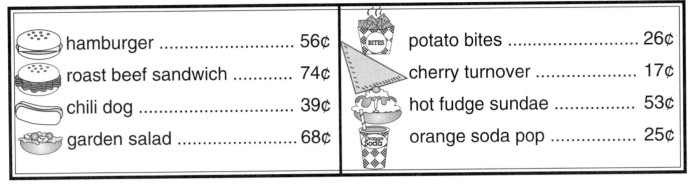

| | |
|---|---|
| hamburger .......................... 56¢ | potato bites .......................... 26¢ |
| roast beef sandwich ............ 74¢ | cherry turnover ..................... 17¢ |
| chili dog .............................. 39¢ | hot fudge sundae ................ 53¢ |
| garden salad ....................... 68¢ | orange soda pop ................. 25¢ |

1. Ricky bought a chili dog and an orange soda pop for lunch. How much did Ricky's lunch cost?

2. Lamar bought a salad for his mother and potato bites for himself. How much did Lamar spend altogether?

3. Megan bought a hamburger and potato bites on the way to dance class. How much did Megan spend in all?

4. Torry ordered a hot fudge sundae and a cherry turnover to go. How much did Torry's order cost?

5. Molly's father bought her a cherry turnover and an orange soda pop after school. How much did Molly's snack cost?

6. Jeff ordered a chili dog for his sister and a hamburger for himself. How much did Jeff spend altogether?

7. Jim and George each bought a roast beef sandwich and a cherry turnover. How much did each boy spend?

8. Anne bought a hamburger and an orange soda. How much did Anne's snack cost?

| Stop 'N' Go Munchies | Stop 'N' Go Munchies | Stop 'N' Go Munchies | Stop 'N' Go Munchies | Stop 'N' Go Munchies | Stop 'N' Go Munchies | Stop 'N' Go Munchies | Stop 'N' Go Munchies |
|---|---|---|---|---|---|---|---|
| 1. | 2. | 3. | 4. | 5. | 6. | 7. | 8. |

**Bonus Box:** How much would it cost if you bought one of every item on the menu? _____

## Answer Key

1. 64¢
2. 94¢
3. 82¢
4. 70¢
5. 42¢
6. 95¢
7. 91¢
8. 81¢

**Bonus Box Answer:** $3.58

Name _____

# Hot Hamburgers To Go!

Read each problem carefully.
Solve each problem on the matching glass below.
Show your work.

1. 26 hamburgers with pickles.
14 hamburgers with onions.
How many more hamburgers
with pickles than with onions?

2. 88 hamburgers on the shelf.
53 hamburgers were sold.
How many hamburgers were
left?

3. Joe cooked 47 super burgers.
Sally cooked 24 mini-burgers.
How many more super burgers
than mini-burgers?

4. 96 hamburgers were eaten.
72 cheeseburgers were eaten.
How many more hamburgers
than cheeseburgers were eaten?

5. 88 hamburgers with catsup.
47 hamburgers with mustard.
How many more hamburgers
with catsup than with mustard?

6. There were 96 cheeseburgers.
The manager took cheese off
26 of them. How many
cheeseburgers were left?

7. 43 double hamburgers.
21 double cheeseburgers.
How many more double
hamburgers than cheeseburgers?

8. 67 hamburgers with the works.
34 were eaten.
How many hamburgers were
left?

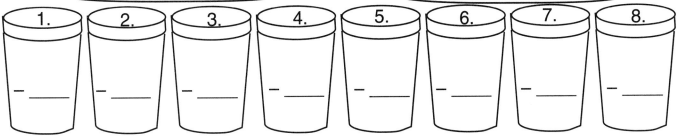

1.    2.    3.    4.    5.    6.    7.    8.

_ _ _ _    _ _ _ _    _ _ _ _    _ _ _ _    _ _ _ _    _ _ _ _    _ _ _ _    _ _ _ _

# How To Use The Corner Decoration Below

Duplicate the corner decoration below for each child. Have each child color and cut out the corner decoration, spread a coat of glue on the space indicated, and attach the decoration behind the upper left corner of his completed math page. Mount students' work on a bulletin board entitled "Here's What's Cooking!"

## Corner Decoration

©The Education Center, Inc.

Glue here.

### Answer Key
1. 12 more
2. 35 hamburgers
3. 23 more
4. 24 more
5. 41 more
6. 70 cheeseburgers
7. 22 more
8. 33 hamburgers

_____'s Merry Meal

Read each problem carefully.
Solve each problem.
Write your answer on the line.

1. 72 Merry Meals have surprise toys. 38 Merry Meals have surprise games. How many more Merry Meals have surprise toys? _____

2. A chicken tidbit Merry Meal costs 93¢. A hamburger Merry Meal costs 77¢. How much more does a chicken tidbit Merry Meal cost? _____

3. After a field trip, three classes stopped at Merry Hut for lunch. The children ordered 45 cheeseburger Merry Meals and 18 hamburger Merry Meals. How many more cheeseburger Merry Meals were ordered? _____

4. The Brooklyn Elementary third-grade classes won the school spirit contest. For their prize they received 52 Merry Meals with milkshakes and 24 Merry Meals with soda pop. How many more Merry Meals with milkshakes than with soda pop? _____

5. A cheeseburger Merry Meal costs 96¢. A fish tidbit Merry Meal costs 89¢. How much more does a cheeseburger Merry Meal cost? _____

6. Megan's Merry Meal has 32 french fries. Matthew's Merry Meal has 41 french fries. How many more french fries does Matthew have?

_____

7. The soccer team needs 22 Merry Meals. The volleyball team needs 14 Merry Meals. How many more Merry Meals does the soccer team need? _____

8. 29 Merry Meals have chocolate chip cookies. 51 Merry Meals have oatmeal cookies. How many more Merry Meals have oatmeal cookies? _____

**Bonus Box:** Cut the worksheet along the dark lines. Fold the worksheet in half to make a Merry Meal box. Then design and color your very own Merry Meal box.

# Materials Needed For Bonus Box

scissors
crayons

Name _____

# Crowin' Time!

Complete the hands on the clocks.
Write the letter of the correct clock by each sentence.

a.

g.

b.

_____ Rex Rooster crows at 6:30 every morning to wake up the pigs.

_____ At 10 o'clock Farmer Ray throws Rex some feed.

h.

_____ Rex reminds the cows to come in at 5:00.

_____ By 12:30 Rex is ready for a nap.

c.

_____ When it is 2 o'clock Rex Rooster is crowing for a snack.

i.

_____ Every day at 11:30 Rex crows just for fun.

d.

_____ Rex's crow at 1:00 means the mailman will be here soon.

_____ The geese come to listen to Rex crow at 3:30.

j.

e.

_____ Rex crows one last time every night at 9 o'clock.

_____ At four-thirty Rex is crowing for dinner.

k.

f.

_____ At 7:00 you can see Rex on top of the barn.

l.

_____ Crowing lessons are at 8:30 each morning for Rex's sons.

**Bonus Box:** On the back of this sheet write down three things that you do every day. Then draw a clock for each thing to show what time you do it. Draw a line to connect each clock to its activity.

## Follow-up Activity

Practice sequencing by having the students cut out the sentences and arrange them in the order of Rex's day. Then they cut out the clocks to match. Glue completed projects on another sheet of paper.

## Background For The Teacher
## Time And Clocks

Long ago people could tell how much time had passed by watching the sun. Shadow clocks, water clocks, sand clocks, and rope clocks were invented to keep track of time. Mechanical clocks began to appear in the late 1200s. Minute and second hands were common by the early 1700s.

The sun's placement in the sky was used to set the time on individual clocks. This resulted in few clocks having the same time. The invention of the *time ball* (a large, hollow, red, metal ball attached to a high pole and lowered at noon) helped people living in the same town synchronize their times. However, this did not help people from town to town agree on the time of day. This was a serious problem for the railroads and their passengers. On November 18, 1883, the railroad took the suggestion of Charles Dowd and established a standard time for the United States. This divided the United States into four time zones, and clocks were set accordingly. Congress legalized this system in 1918. Though altered, these time zones are still in effect today.

Time is kept without the use of a clock in nature. Roosters wake up and crow at sunrise every morning. Some oysters open and close their shells as the tides change. Various plants open their flowers at certain times of the day or night. Scientists know that living organisms have a method of telling time within them and continue to search for new information and explanations.

## Extension Activities

—Practice telling time by doing a time-check count in your classroom. Each time a student looks at a clock or watch to check the time, he must record the time on his paper, along with the reason for checking. Compile lists at the end of the day to see what the most popular time-check times and reasons were!

—This bulletin board entitled "Once Upon A Time" will be a fun free-time activity. Provide each child with a duplicated clock face and an individual time on a slip of paper. Children program their clocks with their times and then write "Once Upon A Time" stories to match. They must mention their times in their stories at least once. Separate the clocks and stories to display. Children visit the bulletin board and match the clocks to the stories with lengths of yarn and pushpins.

—Explore the saying, "I've only got a minute," with your class. Think about things you could do in one minute. Write your name a dozen times? Answer 20 math facts? Say the alphabet backwards? Try it! What could you do in five minutes?

—Have each student bring in his favorite recipe to share. Determine as a class a starting and a stopping time for each recipe. Plan a cooking project as a finale.

| | |
|---|---|
| **k.** | Rex Rooster crows at <u>6:30</u> every morning to wake up the pigs. |
| **c.** | At <u>10 o'clock</u> Farmer Ray throws Rex some feed. |
| **l.** | Rex reminds the cows to come in at <u>5:00</u>. |
| **d.** | By <u>12:30</u> Rex is ready for a nap. |
| **h.** | When it is <u>2 o'clock</u> Rex is crowing for a snack. |
| **f.** | Every day at <u>11:30</u> Rex crows just for fun. |
| **i.** | Rex's crow at <u>1:00</u> means the mailman will be here soon. |
| **j.** | The geese come to listen to Rex crow at <u>3:30</u>. |
| **g.** | Rex crows one last time every night at <u>9 o'clock</u>. |
| **b.** | At <u>four-thirty</u> Rex is crowing for dinner. |
| **a.** | At <u>7:00</u> you can see Rex on top of the barn. |
| **e.** | Crowing lessons are at <u>8:30</u> each morning for Rex's sons. |

Name _____

# Flying Time

Write the times on the lines.
Cross out your answers in the barn.

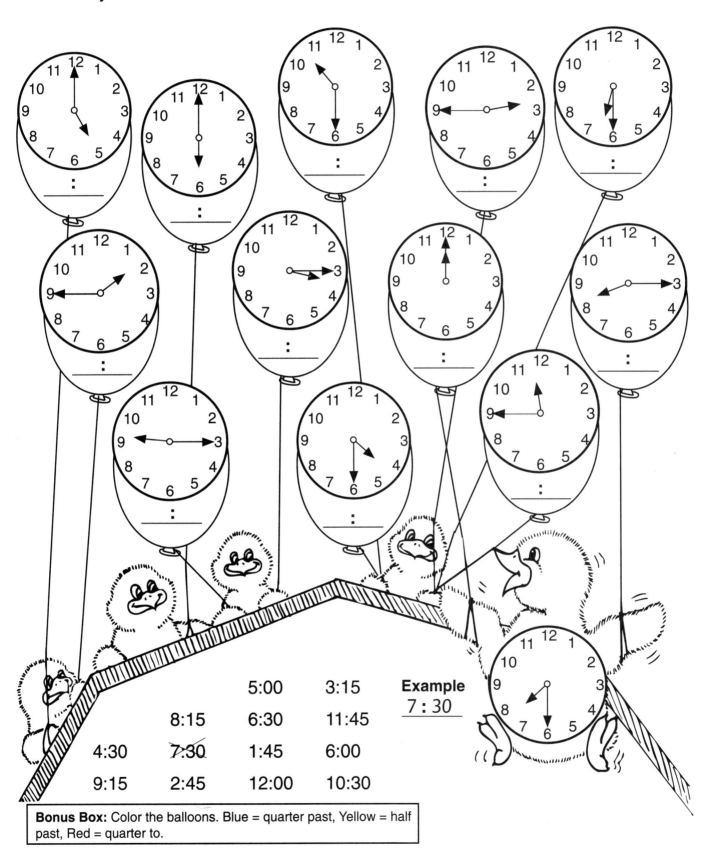

5:00   3:15

8:15   6:30   11:45

**Example**
7 : 30

4:30   7:30   1:45   6:00

9:15   2:45   12:00   10:30

**Bonus Box:** Color the balloons. Blue = quarter past, Yellow = half past, Red = quarter to.

# Extension Activity
## Telling-Time Practice

Duplicate student copies of the clock and the clock hands below. Have each child color and cut out his patterns. Then have the child attach the hands to the clock at the Xs using a brad. Next divide students into pairs. In turn, have each child set his clock and have his partner tell the time.

## Clock Patterns

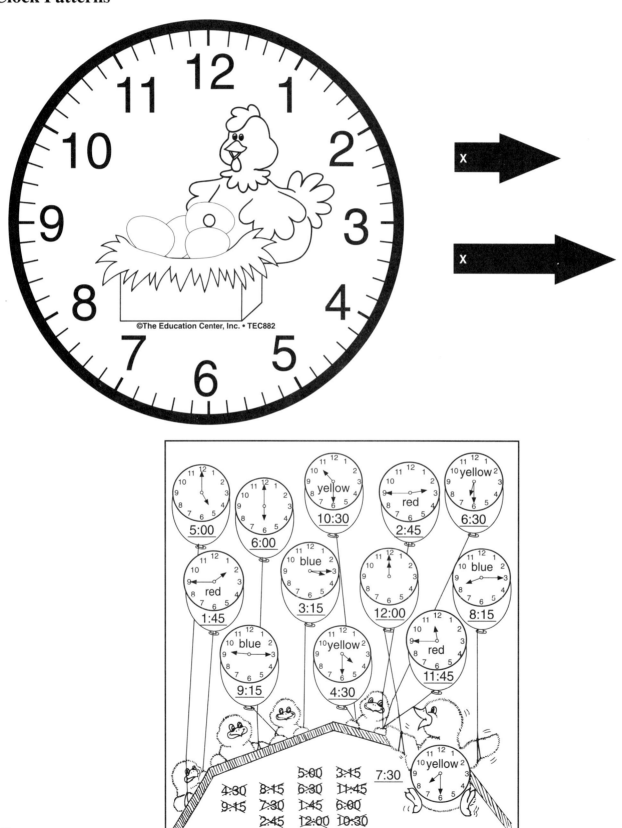

©The Education Center, Inc. • TEC882

Name _____

# Time To Be Choosy

Read the time.
Color two eggs in the same row for each clock.

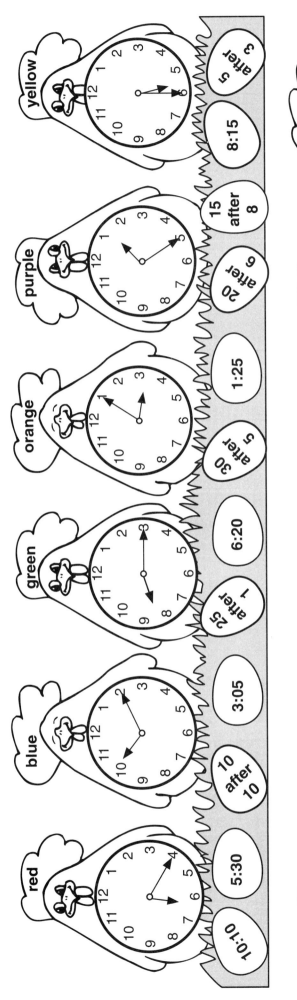

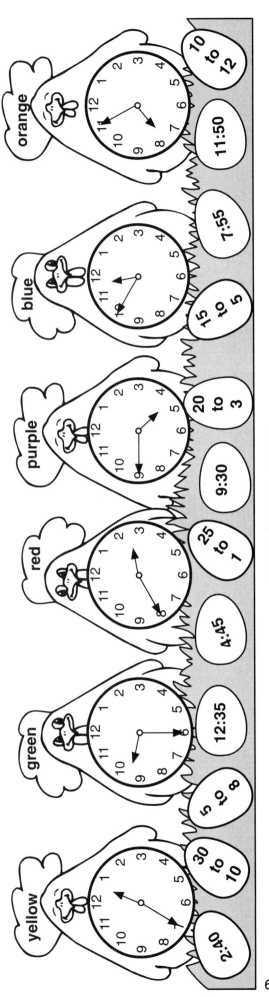

©The Education Center, Inc. • TEC882

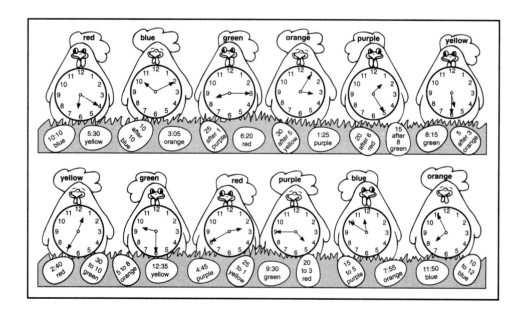

# Every Minute Counts

Read the time.

Fill in the blanks above and below each clock.

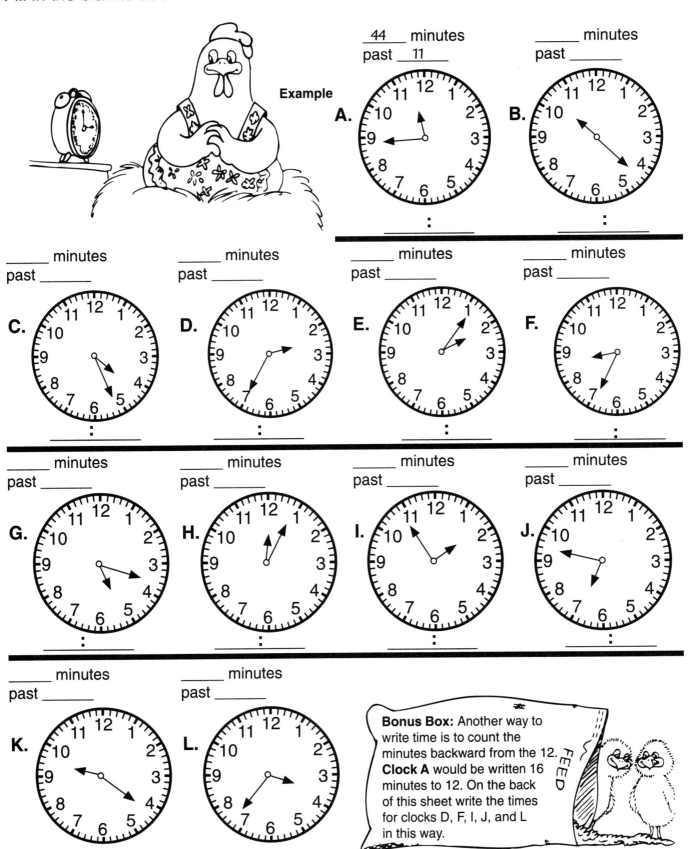

**Example**

_44_ minutes

past _11_

A.

_____ minutes

past _____

B.

___:___

___:___

_____ minutes

past _____

C.

_____ minutes

past _____

D.

_____ minutes

past _____

E.

_____ minutes

past _____

F.

___:___

___:___

___:___

___:___

_____ minutes

past _____

G.

_____ minutes

past _____

H.

_____ minutes

past _____

I.

_____ minutes

past _____

J.

___:___

___:___

___:___

___:___

_____ minutes

past _____

K.

_____ minutes

past _____

L.

**Bonus Box:** Another way to write time is to count the minutes backward from the 12. **Clock A** would be written 16 minutes to 12. On the back of this sheet write the times for clocks D, F, I, J, and L in this way.

FEED

___:___

___:___

# Variation

Provide additional practice by whiting-out and reprogramming
the hands on the clocks.

**Answers to Bonus Box:**

D.  25 minutes to 3
F.  26 minutes to 9
I.  6 minutes to 2
J.  13 minutes to 7
L.  23 minutes to 4

Name _____

# Time To Tell

Read each problem.
Write the time on the line.
Draw the hands on the clock to match.

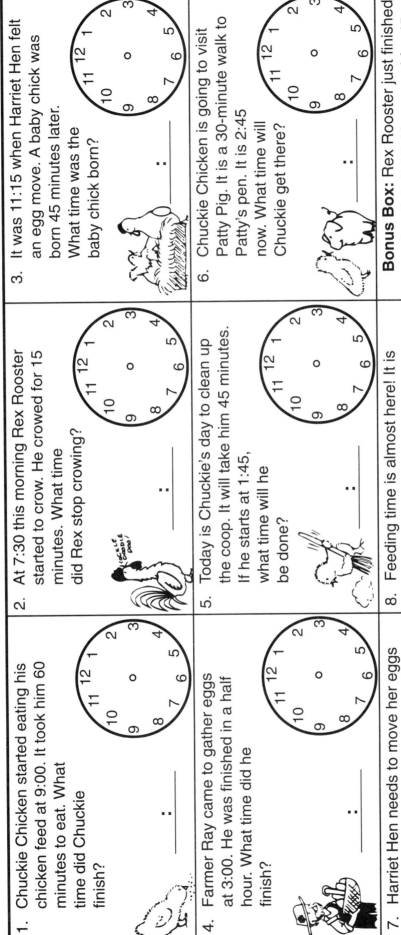

1. Chuckie Chicken started eating his chicken feed at 9:00. It took him 60 minutes to eat. What time did Chuckie finish?

2. At 7:30 this morning Rex Rooster started to crow. He crowed for 15 minutes. What time did Rex stop crowing?

3. It was 11:15 when Harriet Hen felt an egg move. A baby chick was born 45 minutes later. What time was the baby chick born?

4. Farmer Ray came to gather eggs at 3:00. He was finished in a half hour. What time did he finish?

5. Today is Chuckie's day to clean up the coop. It will take him 45 minutes. If he starts at 1:45, what time will he be done?

6. Chuckie Chicken is going to visit Patty Pig. It is a 30-minute walk to Patty's pen. It is 2:45 now. What time will Chuckie get there?

7. Harriet Hen needs to move her eggs around. She will start at 12:00. It will take her one hour and 30 minutes. What time will she be done?

8. Feeding time is almost here! It is 5:15 now. Dinner is in 30 minutes. What time is feeding time?

**Bonus Box:** Rex Rooster just finished crowing. It is 5:15. He crowed for 45 minutes. When did Rex begin to crow?

71

## Variations

— Simplify this worksheet by programming the clocks with the hour hands. Students complete the clock faces by adding the minute hands.

— White-out the Bonus Box and provide written times in an answer key.

## How To Use The Award Below

Duplicate and cut out copies of the award watch below. When a child successfully completes a desired telling-time goal, tape a personalized watch to his wrist. The child may draw hands on his watch to show the desired time.

## Award

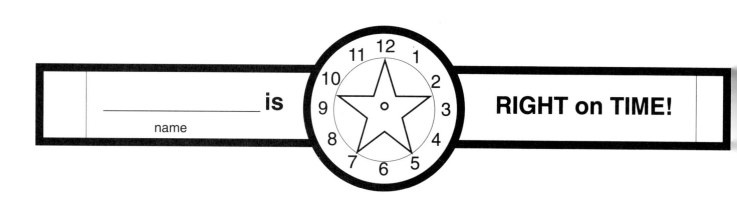

_____ is    **RIGHT on TIME!**
name

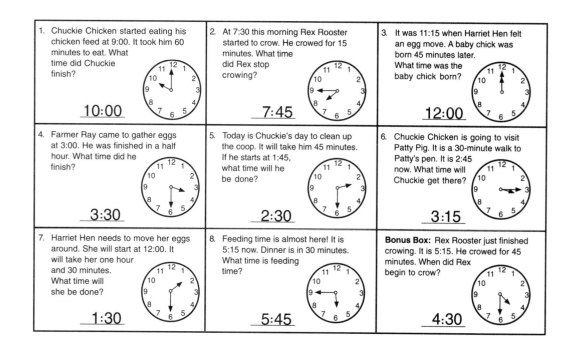

1. Chuckie Chicken started eating his chicken feed at 9:00. It took him 60 minutes to eat. What time did Chuckie finish?

   10:00

2. At 7:30 this morning Rex Rooster started to crow. He crowed for 15 minutes. What time did Rex stop crowing?

   7:45

3. It was 11:15 when Harriet Hen felt an egg move. A baby chick was born 45 minutes later. What time was the baby chick born?

   12:00

4. Farmer Ray came to gather eggs at 3:00. He was finished in a half hour. What time did he finish?

   3:30

5. Today is Chuckie's day to clean up the coop. It will take him 45 minutes. If he starts at 1:45, what time will he be done?

   2:30

6. Chuckie Chicken is going to visit Patty Pig. It is a 30-minute walk to Patty's pen. It is 2:45 now. What time will Chuckie get there?

   3:15

7. Harriet Hen needs to move her eggs around. She will start at 12:00. It will take her one hour and 30 minutes. What time will she be done?

   1:30

8. Feeding time is almost here! It is 5:15 now. Dinner is in 30 minutes. What time is feeding time?

   5:45

**Bonus Box:** Rex Rooster just finished crowing. It is 5:15. He crowed for 45 minutes. When did Rex begin to crow?

   4:30

# Made In The Shade

Look at each clock.
Write the time on the lines below each clock.

**Bonus Box:** On the back of this sheet, draw a clock showing the time school starts in the morning. Write the time under the clock.

©The Education Center, Inc. • TEC882

73

## How To Use Page 73

Duplicate copies of page 73 onto duplicating paper. Have students complete and color their worksheets. Using an X-acto knife, have an adult cut along the dotted lines of the palm leaves. Fold the leaves as shown. Back the worksheets with colorful construction paper and attach to a bulletin board for a tropical display your students are sure to go ape over!

## Extension Activities
## Time Vocabulary Display/Task Cards

— Help your students correctly tell time with this classroom clock display. Duplicate copies of the pattern below onto tagboard. Color, label, cut out, and place beside your classroom clock as shown.

— Duplicate copies of the pattern below onto tagboard. Color and program the task cards with digital times and programmed clocks. Cut apart and place in a string-tie envelope entitled "Time For A Banana Break!" Have students match digital times and clocks.

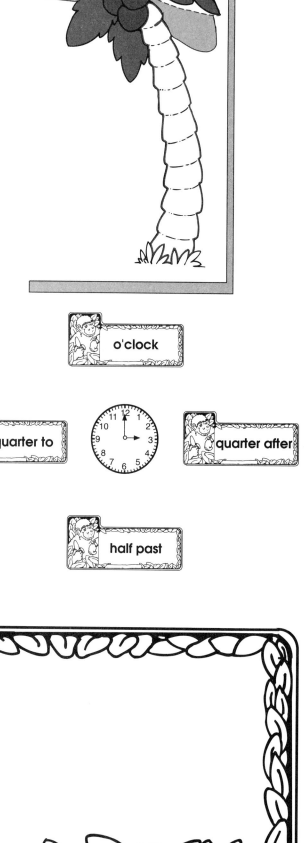

## Pattern

Name _____

# It's A Jungle Out There!

Write the time on the lines below each clock.
Color the leaves light green as you use the answers.

7:30  4:30  10:45

8:00  10:15

2:15  8:15  7:45  2:00  5:45

1:45  3:45  9:30

3:00  2:30

10:30  4:15  1:00  6:15  5:15

**Bonus Box:** Color the remaining leaves dark green.

©The Education Center, Inc. • TEC882

75

## Answer Key for page 73.

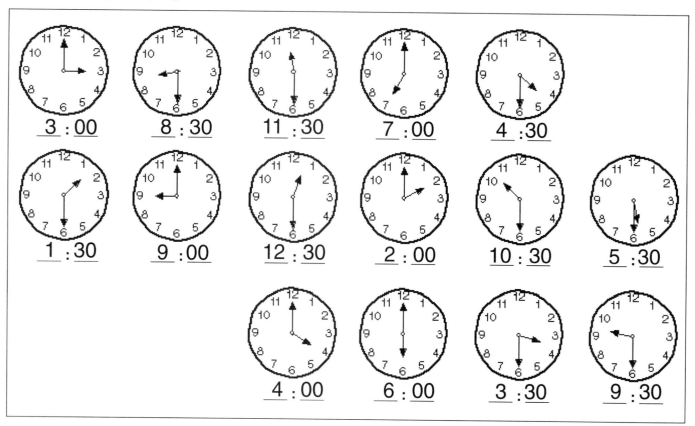

3 : 00   8 : 30   11 : 30   7 : 00   4 : 30

1 : 30   9 : 00   12 : 30   2 : 00   10 : 30   5 : 30

4 : 00   6 : 00   3 : 30   9 : 30

## Answer Key for page 75.

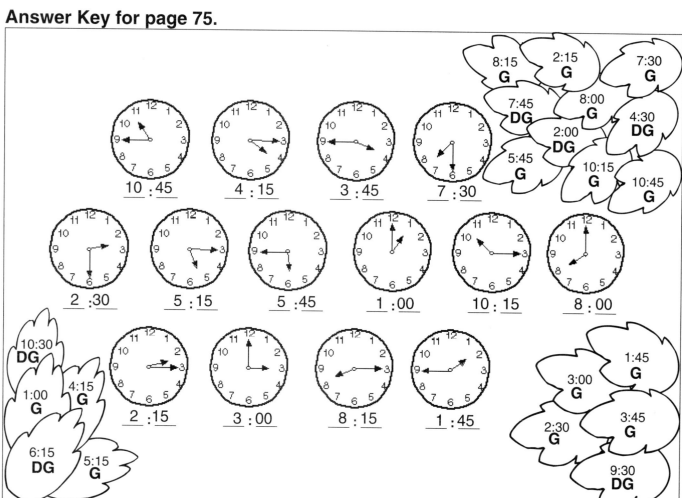

10 : 45   4 : 15   3 : 45   7 : 30

8:15 G   2:15 G   7:30 G
7:45 DG   8:00 G
2:00 DG   4:30 DG
5:45 G   10:15 G   10:45 G

2 : 30   5 : 15   5 : 45   1 : 00   10 : 15   8 : 00

10:30 DG
1:00 G   4:15 G
6:15 DG   5:15 G

2 : 15   3 : 00   8 : 15   1 : 45

1:45 G
3:00 G
2:30 G   3:45 G
9:30 DG

# Jungle Clock Rock

Look at each clock.
Circle the letter beside the correct time.

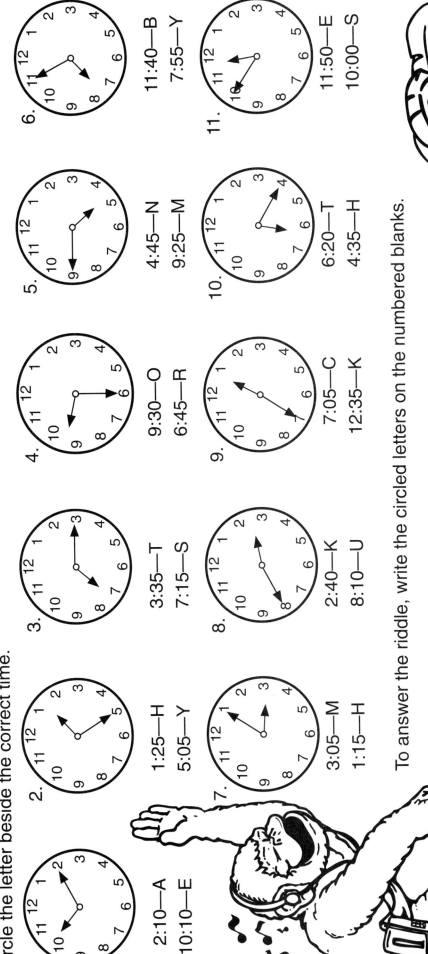

1.
2:10—A
10:10—E

2.
1:25—H
5:05—Y

3.
3:35—T
7:15—S

4.
9:30—O
6:45—R

5.
4:45—N
9:25—M

6.
11:40—B
7:55—Y

7.
3:05—M
1:15—H

8.
2:40—K
8:10—U

9.
7:05—C
12:35—K

10.
6:20—T
4:35—H

11.
11:50—E
10:00—S

To answer the riddle, write the circled letters on the numbered blanks.

## What is an ape's favorite dance step?

___ ___ ___ ___ ___ ___ ___ ___ ___
10  2  11     7  4  5  9  1  6

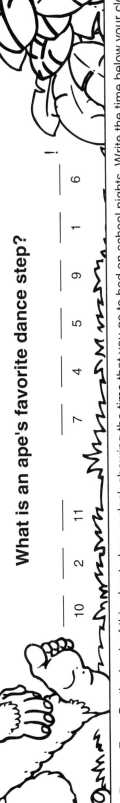

**Bonus Box:** On the back of this sheet, draw a clock showing the time that you go to bed on school nights. Write the time below your clock.

## Answer Key

1. 2:10—A  2. 1:25—H  3. 3:35—T  4. 9:30—O  5. 4:45—N  6. 11:40—B

10:10—E  5:05—Y  7:15—S  6:45—R  9:25—M  7:55—Y

7. 3:05—M  8. 2:40—K  9. 7:05—C  10. 6:20—T  11. 11:50—E

1:15—H  8:10—U  12:35—K  4:35—H  10:00—S

**Answer to riddle:** The Monkey!

# It's Vine Time!

Look at each clock.
Write the time on the lines below the clock.

___ : ___          ___ : ___

8:00–1:30
1:31–5:40
5:41–7:59

Primate Primary School
Vine Swinging Lessons
Jungle Fitness Class

___ : ___          ___ : ___          ___ : ___          ___ : ___

___ : ___          ___ : ___          ___ : ___          ___ : ___

Circle the times Andy is in school.
Draw a box around the times Andy has vine swinging lessons.
Underline the times Andy has jungle fitness class.

# Extension Activity
## Daily Time Checks

Give your students daily time-telling practice. Duplicate copies of the Daily Time Check Slips below. Attach one slip to each student's desk each morning. Then, throughout the day declare, "Time check!" Write the time on your own Daily Time Check sheet while students check the classroom clock and log the time. At the end of the day, check students' times as a group. Your students will enjoy the "game" while enhancing their time-telling skills.

## Daily Time Check Slips

**Daily Time Check**

1. _____
2. _____
3. _____
4. _____
5. _____

12:25

©The Education Center, Inc.

**Daily Time Check**

1. _____
2. _____
3. _____
4. _____
5. _____

12:25

©The Education Center, Inc.

**Daily Time Check**

1. _____
2. _____
3. _____
4. _____
5. _____

12:25

©The Education Center, Inc.

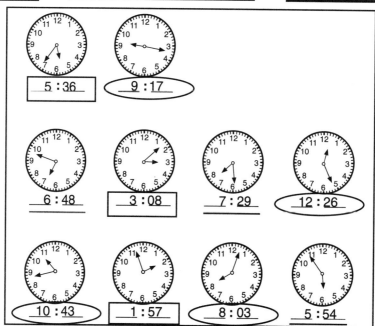

5 : 36    9 : 17

6 : 48    3 : 08    7 : 29    12 : 26

10 : 43    1 : 57    8 : 03    5 : 54

| | | |
|---|---|---|
| 12:45 | | 10:00 |
| 7:15 | | 5:30 |
| 10:30 | | 9:30 |
| 4:15 | | 12:00 |
| 7:30 | | 7:30 |
| 5:45 | | 4:00 |
| 9:15 | | 8:00 |
| 4:45 | | 2:30 |
| 1:00 | | 6:00 |
| 6:15 | | 12:30 |
| 9:45 | | 8:30 |
| 8:45 | | 3:00 |
| 4:30 | | 11:30 |

## Going Ape Over Time

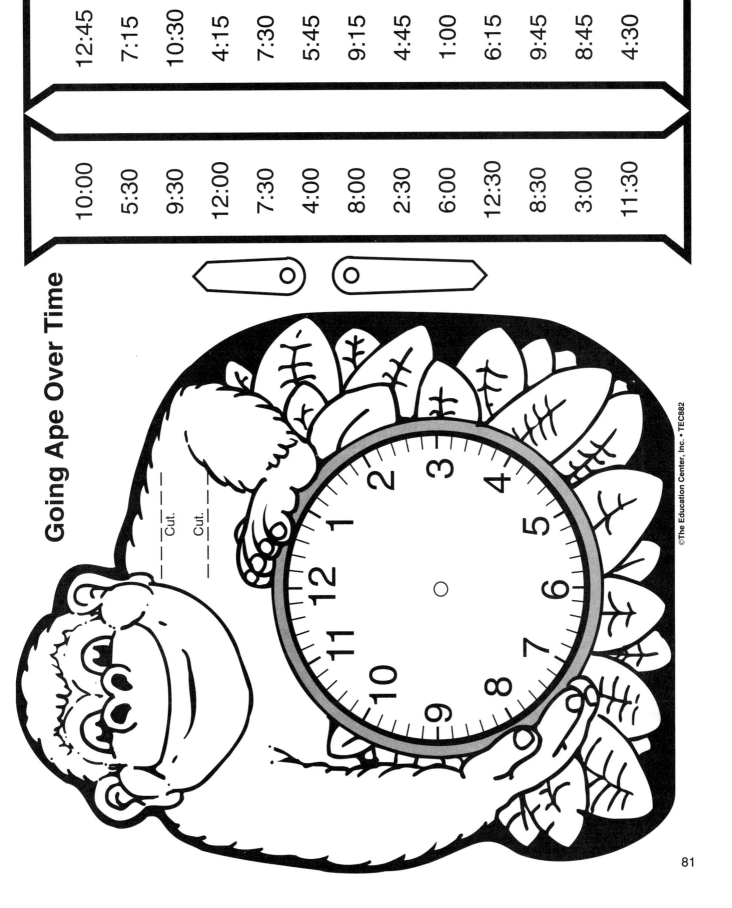

Cut.

Cut.

81

## Materials Needed

crayons
scissors
X-acto knife
brads (1 per student)

## How To Use Page 81

Duplicate copies of page 81 onto tagboard. Have students color and cut out the pieces. Using an X-acto knife, cut the slits for the students. Have students attach the hands to their clocks with brads. Students carefully fold the top notches on the programmed strips to slide them into their tachistoscopes. Have students unfold the notches to keep the strips in place. Change strips as needed for individualized practice.

## Variation

Complete the tachistoscope as described above. Place the tachistoscope at a center entitled "Going Ape Over Time."

## Additional Tachistoscope Strips

To program the open tachistoscope strips below, duplicate onto tagboard and cut out. Insert a strip into the tachistoscope as directed above and pull the strip to the bottom of the tachisto-scope. To program, write a time in the open space on the strip. Pull the strip up one-half inch and continue programming as indicated until the strip is complete.

82                                ©The Education Center, Inc. • TEC882

Name _____

# Pigs In A Blanket

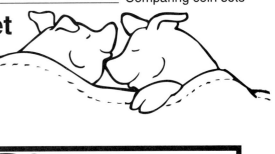

Count the coins on each piggy's blanket.
Write the amount in the blank.
In each pair, color the piggy's blanket
 that shows more money.

# Extension Activity
## Piggy Bank Bonanza/Money Center

Duplicate copies of the piggy bank and coin patterns below onto colorful construction paper. Program the banks with coin sets using rubber stamps. (If desired, program the backs of the banks for self-checking.) Program the coins with corresponding money amounts. Laminate and cut out the banks and coins. Using an X-acto knife, cut along the dotted line on the bank cutouts. Place the pieces in a string-tie envelope decorated as shown. Students match coin sets with money amounts by placing the coins in the slits.

## Patterns

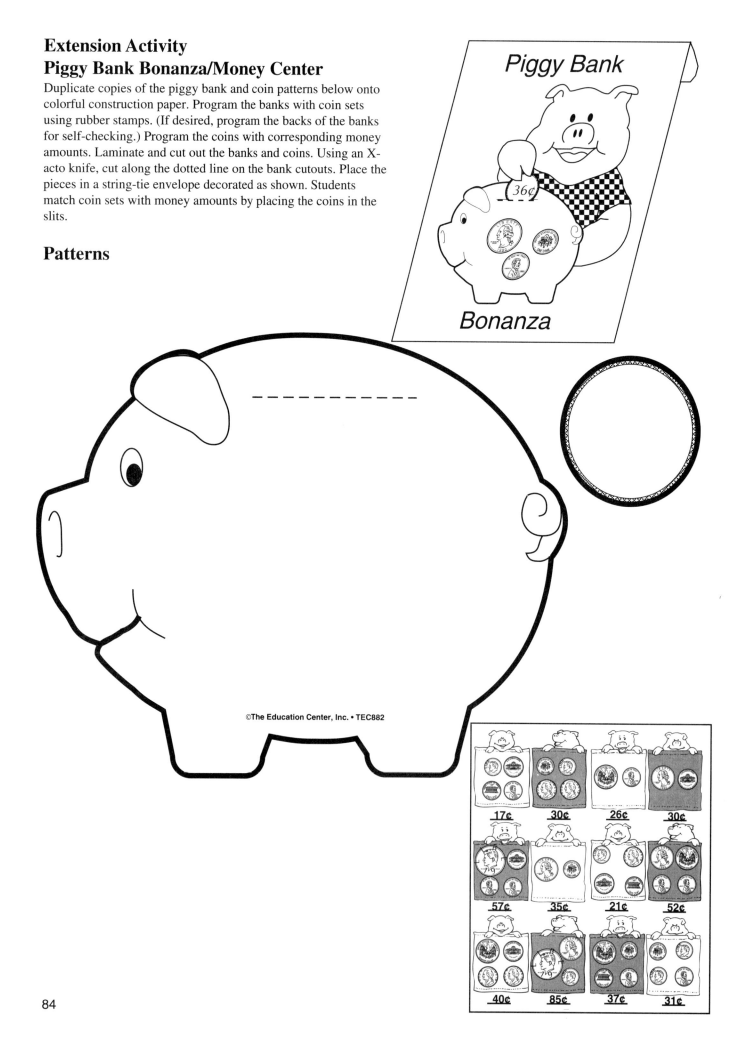

©The Education Center, Inc. • TEC882

Name _____

# Chauncey's Change Purses

Cut and glue each change purse
 by the matching set of coins.

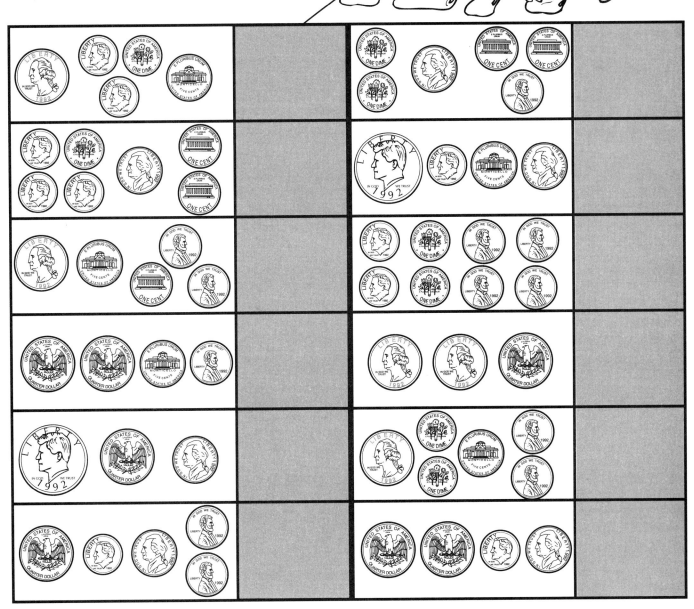

©The Education Center, Inc. • TEC882

| 28¢ | 47¢ | 75¢ | 42¢ | 60¢ | 52¢ |
| 80¢ | 33¢ | 56¢ | 44¢ | 65¢ | 70¢ |

# Books About Money

Use the books from the list below to delight your children and to further inform them about the subject of money.

*Alexander, Who Used To Be Rich Last Sunday* by Judith Viorst (Aladdin Books, 1978)
*If You Made A Million* by David M. Schwartz (Scholastic Inc., 1989)
*The Kids' Complete Guide To Money* by Kathy S. Kyte (Alfred A. Knopf, 1984)
*The Kids Money Book* by Patricia Byers, Patricia Johnson, and Julia Preston (Liberty Books, 1983)

## Answer Key

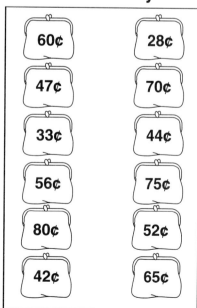

# Put It In The Bank

Name _____

Color the coins needed to fill each piggy bank.

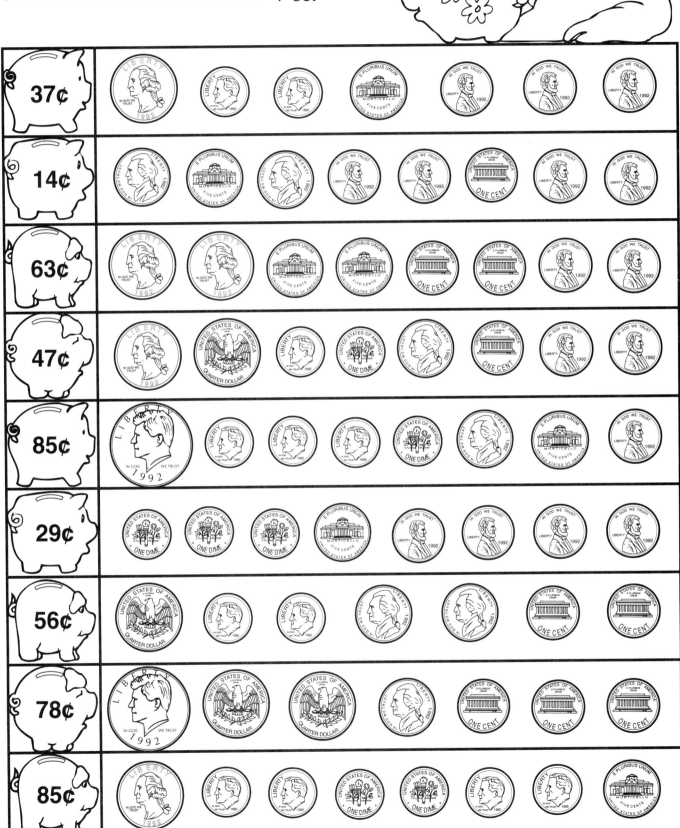

# Answer Key

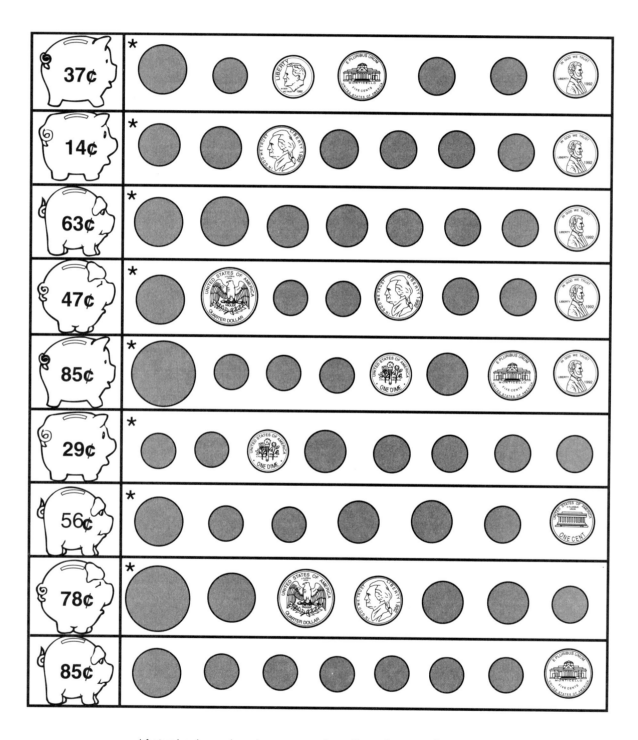

*Actual coins colored may vary since there is more than one coin combination for these amounts.

Name _____

# Penelope's Pig Emporium

Write the amount of money you have in the blank.
Subtract the cost of the item you buy.
Color the amount of money you have left.

| Money You Have | You Buy | Money You Have Left |
|---|---|---|
| $ ._____ | **Slop Savers 25¢** | |
| $ ._____ | *Pretty Piggy* **72¢** *Tail Curler* | |
| $ ._____ | **55¢ a tube** deep-heating "Oink-ment" | |
| $ ._____ | **Corn Meal 40¢** | |
| $ ._____ | **Hoof Shine 34¢** | |
| $ ._____ | **Mud Pack 67¢** | |
| $ ._____ | **Soap 18¢** PIG-B-NEAT | |

**Answer Key**

| Money You Have | Money You Have Left |
|----------------|---------------------|
| $.45 | * |
| $.75 | |
| $.70 | * |
| $.51 | * |
| $.60 | * |
| $.75 | * |
| $.43 | * |

*Actual coins colored may vary since there is more than one coin combination for these amounts.

Name _____

# Buried Treasure

Count the coins in the chests.
Write the amounts on the lids.
Color the chest in each pair that has more money.

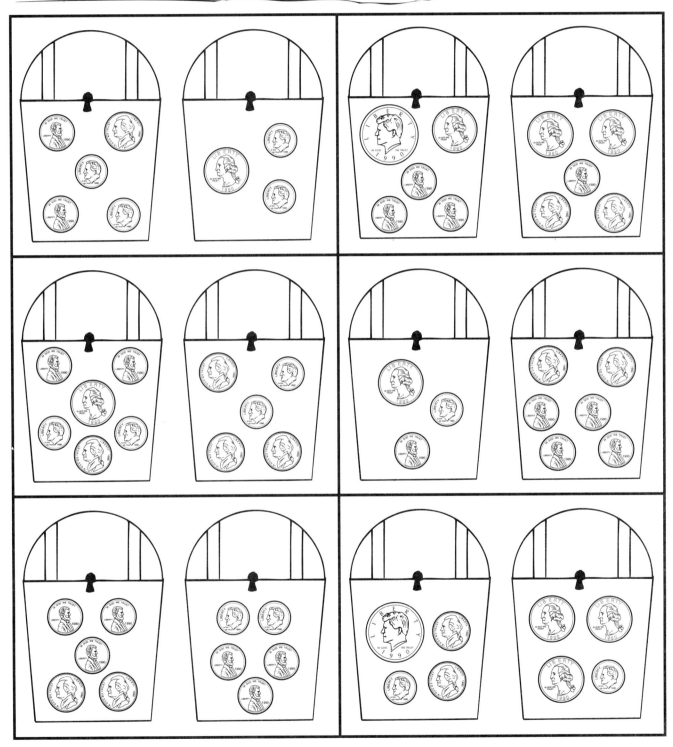

## Background For The Teacher
## Pirates

Pirates were mostly people who wanted to get rich quickly. They attacked ships at sea and raided coastal towns, stealing whatever they could. Piracy was at its peak from the 1500s through the 1700s in the Mediterranean and Caribbean seas.

The lives of pirates, though often referred to as adventurous and romantic, were most likely miserable. Between attacks, pirates fought among themselves and with their crews. They were constantly sought and sometimes jailed by authorities. Many pirates died from diseases or wounds. Some pirates were marooned by their crews and left to die.

Most pirate ships were governed by rules. The crew elected a captain and agreed on the rules and the punishments. A pay scale was established to determine each crew member's share of the stolen goods or booty.

About 1700, pirates began to display flags from their ships. The most common flag, the Jolly Roger, was a white skull and crossbones on a black background. Other pirate flags featured full skeletons, hourglasses, or flaming swords.

## Extension Activities

— Enlarge, color, and laminate the treasure-chest pattern on page 94. Form a flap by cutting on the dotted lines. Display the chest at a center titled "Booty Of The Day." Each day leave an assortment of coins to be counted or a money riddle to solve. Use a wipe-off marker to program the inside of the flap with the answer of the day.

— This money lesson will delight your students. Instruct students to design pirate catalogs, complete with illustrations and prices. After writing five word problems to accompany their catalogs and an answer key, they may staple their completed projects together. On the following day, have students trade catalogs with their classmates and complete the word problems on sheets of paper.

— Let your students help in assigning coin amounts to each letter of the alphabet (penny, nickel, etc.). Display the code in your classroom; then challenge your students to add up the coin amounts of their names, etc. Each morning write a word to be "coined" on the chalkboard. It makes a great entry task and can be tied in with any theme.

— Duplicate the award on page 96 for those students who have shown progress with money skills.

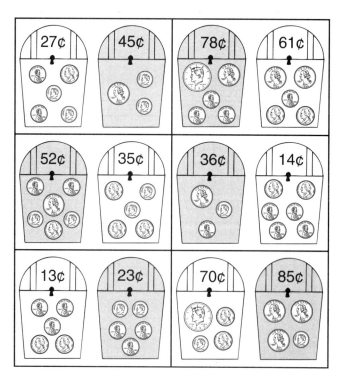

**Answers**
13¢, 14¢, 23¢, 27¢, 35¢, 36¢,
45¢, 52¢, 61¢, 70¢, 78¢, 85¢

Name_____

# "Booty" Shop Bargains

Cut out the bargains.
Glue each bargain by a matching set of coins.

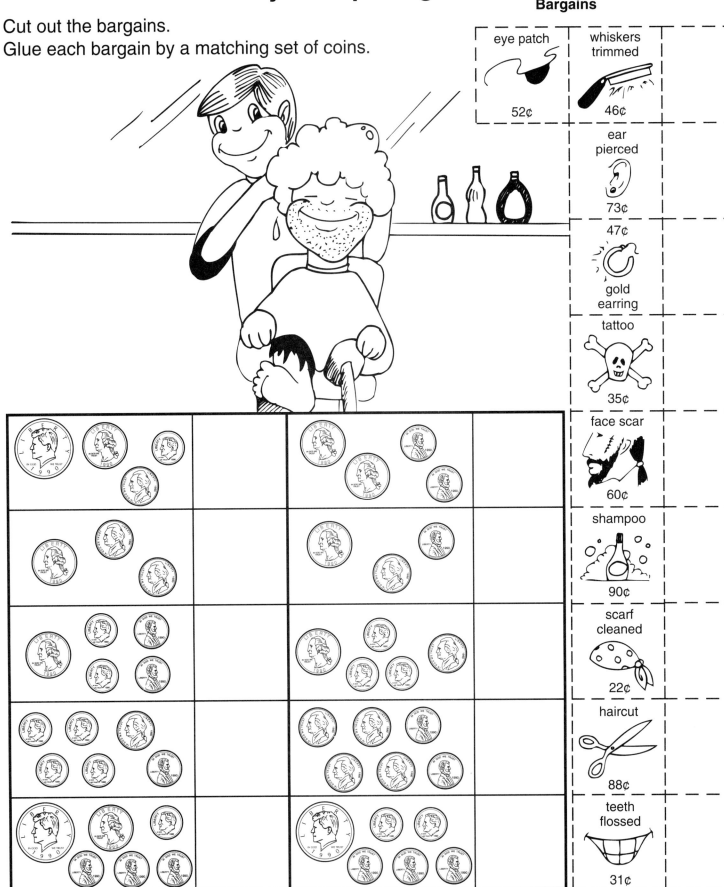

**Bargains**

eye patch
52¢

whiskers trimmed
46¢

ear pierced
73¢

47¢
gold earring

tattoo
35¢

face scar
60¢

shampoo
90¢

scarf cleaned
22¢

haircut
88¢

teeth flossed
31¢

## Variations

— Clip off the "bargains" before duplicating the sheet. Re-write directions, instructing the students to count the coins and write the amounts in the boxes.

— Clip off the "bargains" after duplicating the sheet. Rewrite directions, instructing the students to count the coins and write the amounts in the boxes. Pass out the bargains as a follow-up activity after papers have been corrected.

## Treasure-Chest Pattern

Use with the extension activity on page 92.

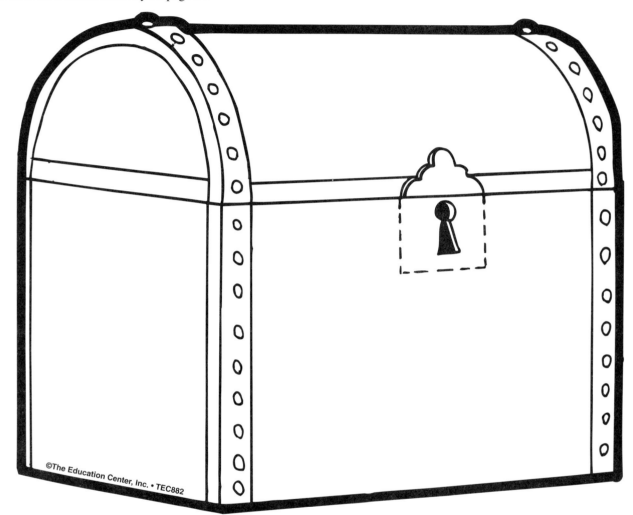

©The Education Center, Inc. • TEC882

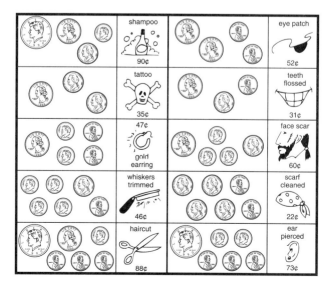

# A Tricky Treasure Map

Fill in the blanks.
The first one is done for you.

| amount | quarters | dimes | nickels | pennies |
|--------|----------|-------|---------|---------|
| 13¢ | 0 | 0 | ■ 2 | 3 |
| 25¢ | 0 | 1 | ■ | 0 |
| 42¢ | 1 | ● | 1 | 2 |
| 24¢ | 0 | 1 | ■ | 4 |
| 60¢ | 1 | ● | 3 | 0 |
| 56¢ | 1 | 2 | 1 | ▼ |
| 40¢ | 0 | 2 | ■ | 5 |
| 32¢ | 0 | 2 | ■ | 2 |
| 78¢ | ▲ | 2 | 1 | 3 |
| 37¢ | 0 | ● | 5 | 2 |
| 21¢ | 0 | 1 | ■ | 1 |
| 65¢ | 2 | 0 | ■ | 5 |
| 51¢ | 0 | ● | 2 | 1 |
| 16¢ | 0 | 0 | ■ | 1 |
| 28¢ | 1 | 0 | 0 | ▼ |

**Bonus Box:** Check your treasure map. Total the coin amounts for each symbol:
▲ = 50¢, ● = 80¢, ■ = 95¢, ▼ = 9¢.

## Variation

White-out the numbers of coins, the symbols on the treasure map, and the Bonus Box. Reprogram as desired.

| amount | quarters | dimes | nickels | pennies |
|--------|----------|-------|---------|---------|
| 13¢ | 0 | 0 | ■ 2 | 3 |
| 25¢ | 0 | 1 | ■ 3 | 0 |
| 42¢ | 1 | ● 1 | 1 | 2 |
| 24¢ | 0 | 1 | ■ 2 | 4 |
| 60¢ | 1 | ● 2 | 3 | 0 |
| 56¢ | 1 | 2 | 1 | ▼ 6 |
| 40¢ | 0 | 2 | ■ 3 | 5 |
| 32¢ | 0 | 2 | ■ 2 | 2 |
| 78¢ | ▲ 2 | 2 | 1 | 3 |
| 37¢ | 0 | ● 1 | 5 | 2 |
| 21¢ | 0 | 1 | ■ 2 | 1 |
| 65¢ | 2 | 0 | ■ 2 | 5 |
| 51¢ | 0 | ● 4 | 2 | 1 |
| 16¢ | 0 | 0 | ■ 3 | 1 |
| 28¢ | 1 | 0 | 0 | ▼ 3 |

# YO, HO, HO!

_____

has discovered a
"wealth"
of money skills!

_____
Teacher

_____
Date

©The Education Center, Inc. • TEC882

Name _____

# Pirate Purchases

Write the amount of money the pirate has.
Color the amount of money left after the purchase.

| Money pirate has | Purchase | Money left |
|---|---|---|
| $ ____.____ | $.34 | |
| $ ____.____ | $.70 | |
| $ ____.____ | $.50 | |
| $ ____.____ | $.45 | |
| $ ____.____ | $.62 | |
| $ ____.____ | $.25 | |
| $ ____.____ | $.71 | |

# Variation

Provide additional practice by whiting-out and reprogramming the purchase prices.

| Money pirate has | Purchase | Money left |
|---|---|---|
| $ .55 | $.34 | |
| $ .85 | $.70 | |
| $ .55 | $.50 | |
| $ .66 | $.45 | |
| $ .75 | $.62 | |
| $ .37 | $.25 | |
| $ .75 | $.71 | |

Name_____

# Inch By Inch With Ivan

Use an inch ruler.
Measure the length of each leaf.
Write the length in the box.

☐ inches

☐ inches        ☐ inch

☐ inches

☐ inches

☐ inches

Measure each line segment in inches.
Write each length in the ◯ .

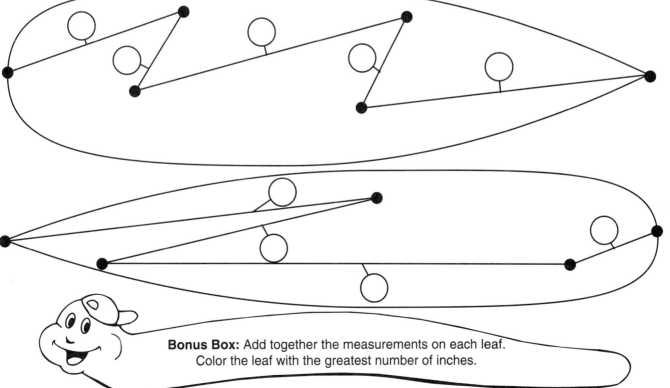

**Bonus Box:** Add together the measurements on each leaf.
Color the leaf with the greatest number of inches.

## Variation

Have Ivan the Inchworm help your students with their measurement skills. Duplicate the ruler below on tagboard for each student. Have each student cut out and glue his ruler, then use it for the measurement activities on pages 99 and 101.

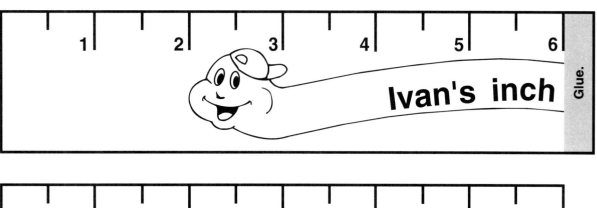

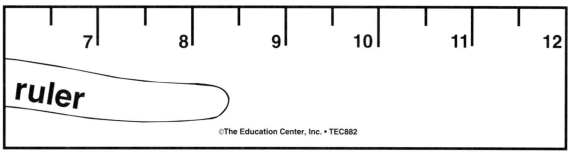

©The Education Center, Inc. • TEC882

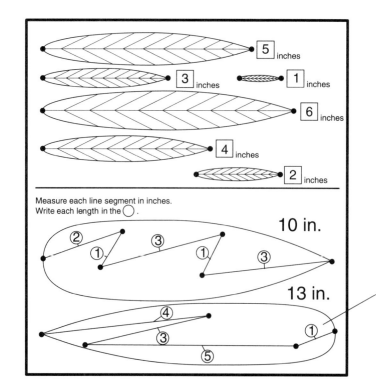

Measurement: half inch

# Ivan Inches Along

Read each step below.
Connect the dots with a straight line.
Measure each line segment.
Write the length in the blank.

**Start**

1. Ivan went to school. _____ inches

2. After school he played baseball. _____ inches

3. Then he went to the ice-cream shop. _____ inches

4. Ivan went to Eddie's house. _____ inches

5. Next he went to the library. _____ inches

6. He tried to chase a butterfly. _____ inches

7. Then he played in a mud puddle. _____ inches

8. Ivan found a penny. _____ inches

9. He ate a tasty leaf. _____ inch

10. Then he took a nap in the sun. _____ inches

**Bonus Box:** Add the measurements to find out how far Ivan crawled.
(Hint: ½ inch + ½ inch = 1 inch) Ivan crawled _____ inches.

©The Education Center, Inc. • TEC882

101

## Additional Activity

Have students estimate the lengths of several small classroom objects. Then have students measure the objects to the nearest inch and to the nearest half inch. Compare the measurements with the estimations. Have students brainstorm a list of activities that require exact measurements such as building a house, making a dress, or measuring a first down in a football game. Then have students brainstorm a second list of things that require only estimated measurements.

## Game Cards

Use with the game on page 106.

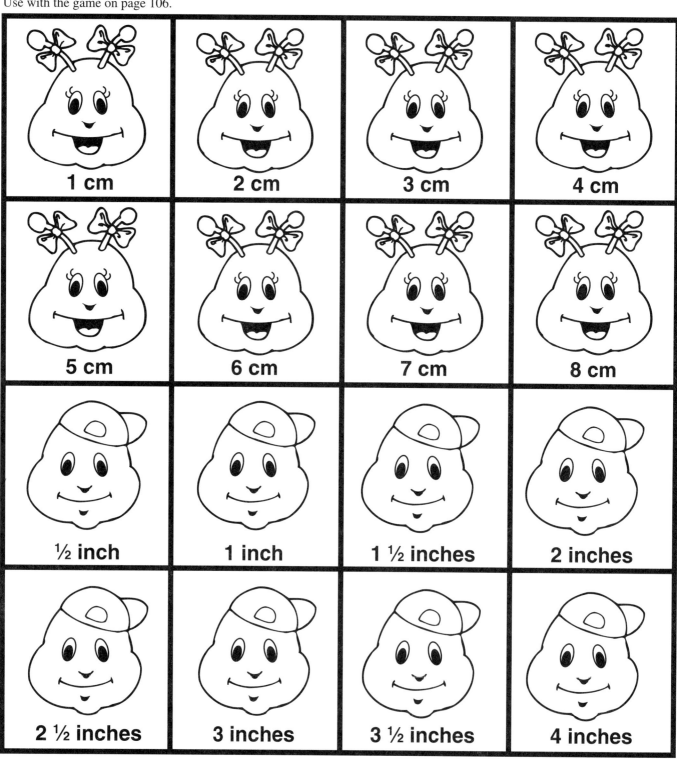

| | | | |
|---|---|---|---|
| 1 cm | 2 cm | 3 cm | 4 cm |
| 5 cm | 6 cm | 7 cm | 8 cm |
| ½ inch | 1 inch | 1 ½ inches | 2 inches |
| 2 ½ inches | 3 inches | 3 ½ inches | 4 inches |

©The Education Center, Inc. • TEC882

# Centimeters With Cindy

Use a centimeter ruler.
Measure the length of each leaf.
Write the length in the box.

☐ cm

☐ cm

☐ cm

☐ cm

☐ cm

☐ cm

Measure each line segment in centimeters.
Write each length in the ◯ .

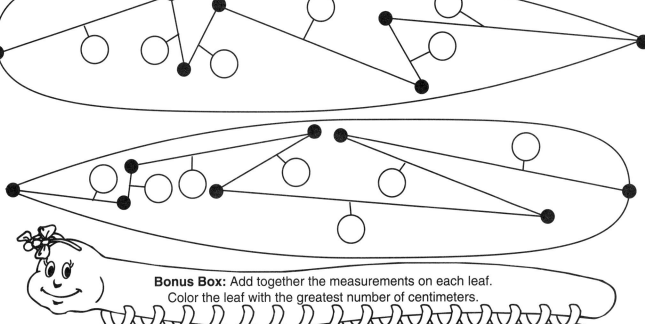

**Bonus Box:** Add together the measurements on each leaf.
Color the leaf with the greatest number of centimeters.

# Variation

Cindy the Centipede adds certain delight to your students' centimeter practice. Duplicate the ruler below on tagboard for each student. Have each student cut out and glue his ruler, then use it for the measurement activities on pages 103 and 105.

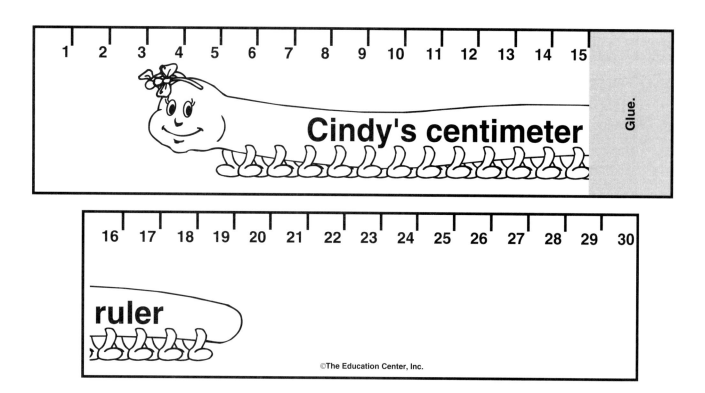

Cindy's centimeter ruler

©The Education Center, Inc.

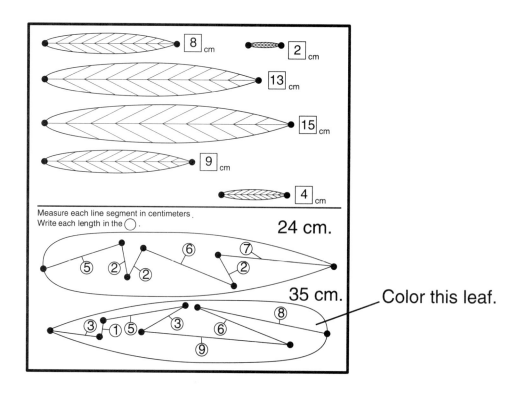

Name _____

# Measuring Up

Fill in the chart.
Guess the length of each object.
Measure to find the length.

1     2     4

| Things to measure in inches: | My guess: | My measurement: | Color a ☺ for each correct guess. |
|---|---|---|---|
| my pencil | _____ inches | _____ inches | ☺ |
| a crayon | _____ inches | _____ inches | ☺ |
| my thumb | _____ inches | _____ inches | ☺ |
| a pair of scissors | _____ inches | _____ inches | ☺ |
| my hand | _____ inches | _____ inches | ☺ |

3  4  5  6  7  8  9  10  11  12  13  14

| Things to measure in centimeters: | My guess: | My measurement: | Color a ☺ for each correct guess. |
|---|---|---|---|
| my pencil | _____ cm | _____ cm | ☺ |
| a crayon | _____ cm | _____ cm | ☺ |
| my thumb | _____ cm | _____ cm | ☺ |
| a pair of scissors | _____ cm | _____ cm | ☺ |
| my hand | _____ cm | _____ cm | ☺ |

# Extension Activities
## Linear Measurement

Jump into linear measurement with both feet—even a whole classroom full of feet! Ask students to guess the combined length of every student's right foot. Have students write their guesses on slips of paper. Divide your students into pairs; then have each student measure his partner's right foot. Have students record their measurements on a class graph. As a group, add the measurements to find the total length. Then read aloud the students' guesses to determine whose estimate was the closest.

## Materials For One Game

copy of game cards on page 102
crayons
scissors
resealable plastic bag
copy of game markers below
two lengths of yarn
tape
inch ruler (See page 100.)
centimeter ruler (See page 104.)

## Measurement Game

Playing this game gives your students added measuring fun!

Divide students into groups of two, three, or four. Provide each group with a game. To make a game, duplicate the game cards on page 102 on white construction paper. Have students color the cards, if desired; then cut them out and store the cards in a resealable plastic bag. Duplicate a game marker below for each child in the group. Allow students to color their game markers. Provide each group with two lengths of yarn, an inch ruler, a centimeter ruler, and tape. Position one length of yarn vertically on a tabletop or on the floor. Secure the ends with tape. Position the second length of yarn as shown (approximately 36 inches away). Secure the ends of the yarn with tape. To begin play, place each player's marker on the first length of yarn. Player 1 draws a card from the plastic bag. He uses the appropriate ruler to measure the distance indicated on the card, starting at the yarn he's on and measuring toward the second length of yarn. Then he moves his game marker accordingly. Return the card to the plastic bag. Players continue, in turn, in the same manner. The first player to reach the second yarn length is the winner.

## Game Markers

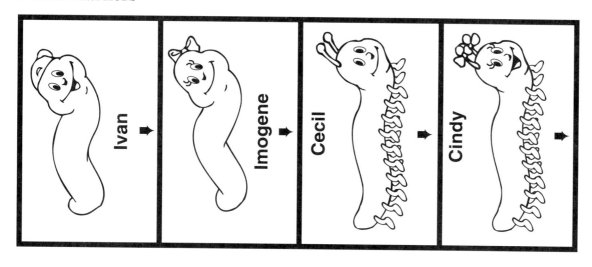

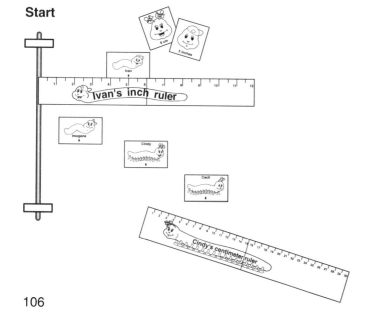

# Champion Chewers

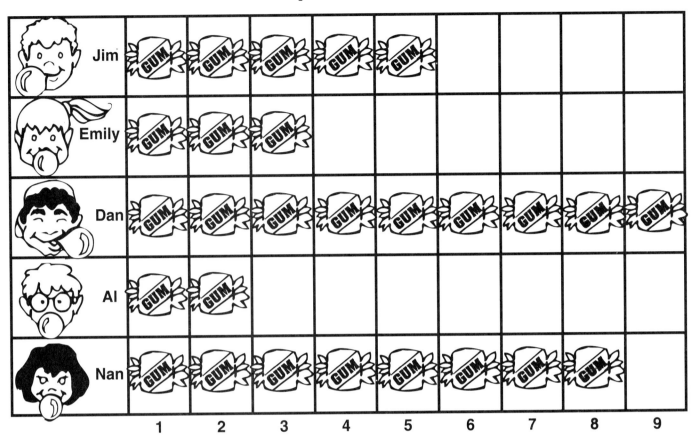

Read the graph. Answer the questions.

1. Who chewed the most pieces of gum? _____

2. Who chewed the fewest pieces of gum? _____

3. How many pieces did Jim and Al chew altogether? _____

4. How many pieces did Emily, Al, and Nan chew altogether? _____

5. How many more pieces did Dan chew than Nan? _____

6. How many more pieces did Jim chew than Emily? _____

7. How many fewer pieces did Emily chew than Nan? _____

8. How many fewer pieces did Jim chew than Dan? _____

9. Who chewed 5 pieces of gum? _____

10. Who chewed 8 pieces of gum? _____

**Bonus Box:** Create a new kind of bubble gum. On the back of this sheet, draw a picture of the gum and write three sentences about it.

# Extension Activity
## Charts And Graphs Learning Center

Help strengthen students' graphing skills with this fun learning center activity. Duplicate several copies of the cards below and on page 110. Cut out the cards and program each card with information and questions (see the illustration). Program the backs of the cards for self-checking. Store the cards in an envelope and place the envelope at a table along with paper and pencils. To use the center, each student takes a graph card from the envelope, answers the questions on a sheet of paper, and turns the card over to check.

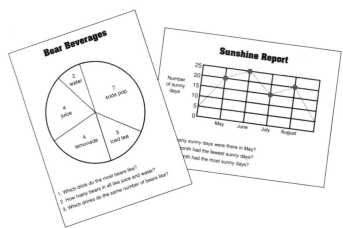

## Cards

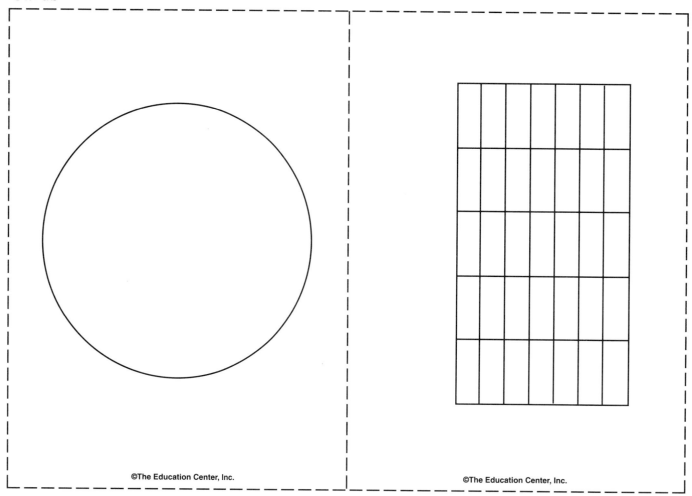

©The Education Center, Inc.

©The Education Center, Inc.

## Answer Key

1. Dan
2. Al
3. 7
4. 13
5. 1 more
6. 2 more
7. 5 fewer
8. 4 fewer
9. Jim
10. Nan

Name _____

# Gum Lovers Graph

Fill in the graph. Complete the sentences.

**Kinds Of Bubble Gum**

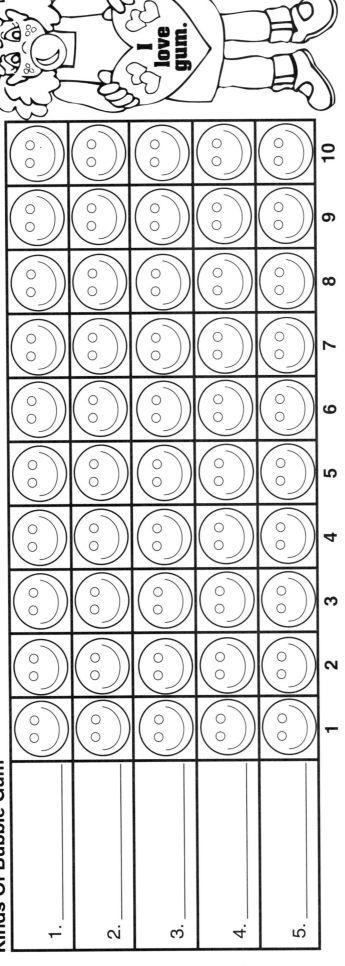

1. _____
2. _____
3. _____
4. _____
5. _____

1 2 3 4 5 6 7 8 9 10

1. Our class liked _____ gum the most.

2. Our class liked _____ gum the least.

3. More children liked _____ gum than _____ gum.

4. Less children liked _____ gum than _____ gum.

5. How many children liked gum number 1 and gum number 4? _____

6. How many children liked gum number 2? _____

**Bonus Box:** Imagine that you blew a bubble so big that you floated away. On the back of this sheet, write about your adventures.

# How To Use Page 109

As a class, choose five kinds of bubble gum. Have each child list the names in the same order down the side of his graph. Then conduct a survey to find out which gum each child most prefers. To do this, have each child stand, one at a time, and tell which of the five kinds of gum is his favorite. As each child names his favorite kind of gum, have the other children color in a smile in the appropriate row on their graphs. If desired, have the children write the child's name on each smile that they color to keep track of the responses. When all of the children have named their favorite kinds of bubble gum, have them answer the questions at the bottom of their worksheets.

## Cards

Use with the extension activity on page 108.

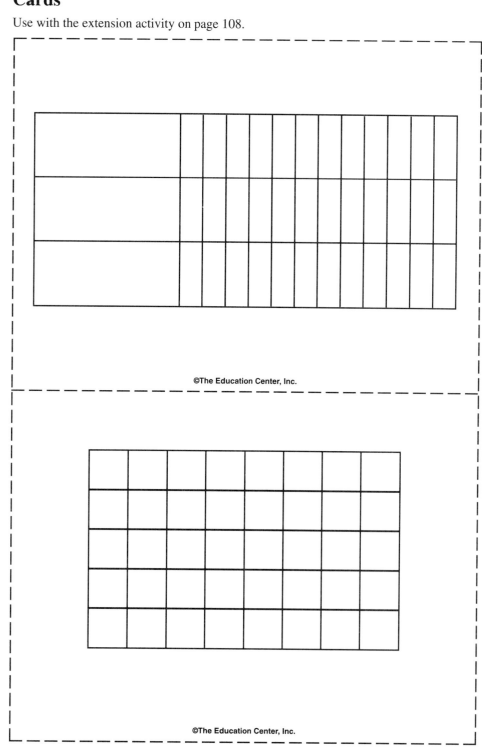

©The Education Center, Inc.

©The Education Center, Inc.

Name _____

## On The Ball

Color the gumballs.
Draw a tally mark for each one.

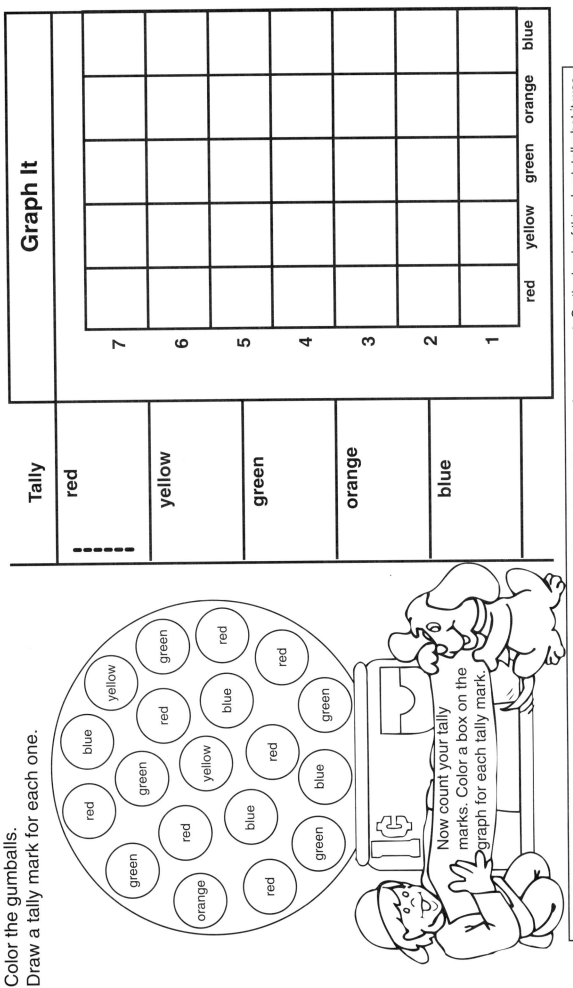

### Graph It

| | red | yellow | green | orange | blue |
|---|---|---|---|---|---|
| **Tally** | | | | | |
| red | ------ | | | | |
| yellow | | | | | |
| green | | | | | |
| orange | | | | | |
| blue | | | | | |

7
6
5
4
3
2
1

red   yellow   green   orange   blue

Now count your tally marks. Color a box on the graph for each tally mark.

**Bonus Box:** Imagine that you put your money in a gumball machine and something amazing came out. On the back of this sheet, tell what it was and what happened.

©The Education Center, Inc. • TEC882

111

# How To Use Page 111

Before assigning page 111 to your students, explain how to tally information. On the board, tally your students' favorite foods or colors. Then give each child a copy of page 111, and briefly explain that they will color and then tally the colors of gumballs before completing the graph. Point out that one tally mark is given so they will need to trace over it.

**Answer Key**

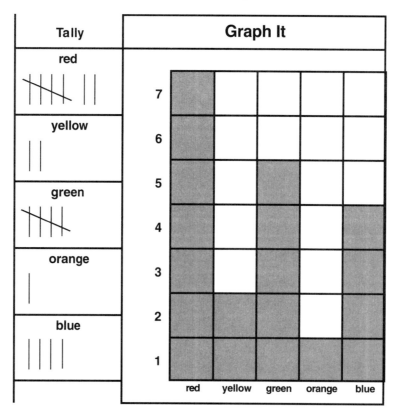

Name _____

# Farmer Fred's Pets

| Farm Pets | | | | | | | | | |
|-----------|---|---|---|---|---|---|---|---|---|
| **Pigs** | 🐷 | 🐷 | 🐷 | 🐷 | 🐷 | | | | |
| **Cows** | 🐮 | 🐮 | 🐮 | | | | | | |
| **Sheep** | 🐑 | 🐑 | 🐑 | 🐑 | 🐑 | 🐑 | 🐑 | 🐑 | 🐑 | 🐑 |
| **Horses** | 🐴 | 🐴 | | | | | | | |
| **Geese** | 🦢 | 🦢 | 🦢 | 🦢 | 🦢 | 🦢 | | | |
| **Goats** | 🐐 | 🐐 | 🐐 | 🐐 | 🐐 | 🐐 | 🐐 | 🐐 | 🐐 |

Each picture equals one animal.

Answer the questions.
Use the graph.

1.  Which animal does Farmer Fred have the least of? _____

2.  Which animal does Farmer Fred have the most of? _____

3.  Which animal does Farmer Fred have six of? _____

4.  Which animal does Farmer Fred have ten of? _____

5.  How many goats and sheep does Farmer Fred have altogether? _____

6.  How many cows, pigs, and horses does Farmer Fred have altogether? _____

7.  Which animal does Farmer Fred have more of—sheep or goats? _____

8.  Which animal does Farmer Fred have less of—pigs or horses? _____

**Bonus Box:** How many animals in the graph have two legs? _____

# Background For The Teacher
## Pets

You name the animal, it's probably been a pet. People have tamed tigers, tarantulas, elephants, and other exotic creatures. By and large, however, humans confine their tastes to certain types of animals: dogs, cats, birds, fish, rodents, and reptiles/amphibians.

Over 150 million dogs live on earth, of which 30 million reside in the United States. Worldwide, there are 400 different dog pedigrees; within the United States, 100 pedigrees. Dogs have been useful to humans during their estimated 10,000-year association: they hunt, guard, race, and even search for illegal drugs.

Cats, on the other hand, have only been domesticated for 4,000 years. Long-haired Persians and shorthairs are the two basic categories of cats.

The interest in birds as pets is surging, despite severe import restrictions on some of the more exotic types. Birds of all types are good pets because of their singing, talking, or affectionate nature.

Fish are widely popular pets. They're modestly priced and easily cared for. Fish differ dramatically in appearance, swimming habits, and even in personalities.

Domesticated rodents are common pets. Pets within this family are white rats, guinea pigs, mice, hamsters, and gerbils. These animals are generally curious, intelligent, and fast to reproduce! Rabbits, though technically not rodents, are similar in these characteristics.

# Extension Activities
## Graphing

— As a group, brainstorm different types of pets that are appropriate for the classroom. Have students cast votes for the pet they would prefer to have as a class pet. Then, as a group, make a pictograph or bar graph showing the results of the vote. After completing the graph, ask the students questions about it, such as: Which pet was the most popular? The least popular? Which pet received more votes—the _____ or the _____?

— Imagination is the key to this activity. Provide students with construction paper, glue, scissors, and old magazines. Have students find and cut out pictures of animals. Then have students create new animals from the pictures they find! Have students cut out different parts of the animals and glue them together on their papers to create new animals. Challenge students to create names for their new animals. For instance, a student might glue together a cat's tail, a bird's body, a dog's head, and a dinosaur's feet, and name it a "dinogcattweeter." Once finished, have students vote on the five most unusual new animals. As a group, graph student votes. Then have students write questions about the graph on 3" x 5" index cards. Place the graph and cards at a center entitled "Graph-animals." If desired, provide an answer key for self-checking.

## Answer Key

1. horses
2. sheep
3. geese
4. sheep
5. 19
6. 10
7. sheep
8. horses

**Bonus Box Answer:** 6

Name _____

# Class Pets

Complete the pictograph.
Each ☺ equals one animal.
Use the information bank.

**Information Bank**

| cats | 4 |
|------|---|
| dogs | 6 |
| fish | 5 |
| birds | 3 |
| rabbits | 1 |
| turtles | 2 |

**Class Pets**

| | | | | | | |
|---|---|---|---|---|---|---|
| Cats | | | | | | |
| Dogs | | | | | | |
| Fish | | | | | | |
| Birds | | | | | | |
| Rabbits | | | | | | |
| Turtles | | | | | | |

**Answer Key**

| Class Pets | | | | | | |
|---|---|---|---|---|---|---|
| Cats | ☺ | ☺ | ☺ | ☺ | | |
| Dogs | ☺ | ☺ | ☺ | ☺ | ☺ | ☺ |
| Fish | ☺ | ☺ | ☺ | ☺ | ☺ | |
| Birds | ☺ | ☺ | ☺ | | | |
| Rabbits | ☺ | | | | | |
| Turtles | ☺ | ☺ | | | | |

# What's New At The Zoo?

Answer the questions.
Use the bar graph.

## New At The Zoo

Number Of Animals

| 12 | | | | | | |
| 11 | | | | | | |
| 10 | | | | | | Skunks |
| 9 | | | Ferrets | | | |
| 8 | | | | | | |
| 7 | | | | | | |
| 6 | | | | Tigers | | |
| 5 | | Pythons | | | | |
| 4 | | | | | | |
| 3 | | | | | | Parrots |
| 2 | Monkeys | | | | | |
| 1 | | | | | | |
| 0 | | | | | | |

Monkeys   Pythons   Ferrets   Tigers   Skunks   Parrots

1. Which animal did the zoo receive the most of?_____

2. Which animal did the zoo receive less of: ferrets or skunks? _____

3. How many skunks and ferrets did the zoo receive altogether? _____

4. Which animal did the zoo receive least of? _____

5. There are five of which animal?_____

6. Which animal did the zoo receive more of: tigers or monkeys? _____

7. The zoo received ten of which animal?_____

**Bonus Box:** If you could have one of the zoo's new animals, which one would you choose? Write your answer on the back of this sheet.

# Extension Activity
## Class Graphs

Involve your students in creating a variety of graphs about themselves. Encourage students to dictate their responses as you create the following graphs on sheets of poster board: a bar graph of birthdays, a line graph of favorite foods, a Venn diagram of family pets (see the illustrations). Discuss each graph with your students and then display them for all to see.

**Favorite Foods Line Graph**

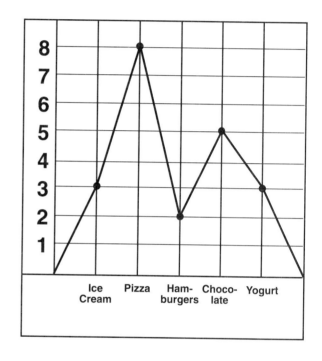

**Birthday Line Graph**

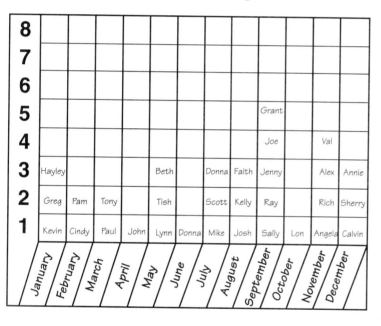

| | January | February | March | April | May | June | July | August | September | October | November | December |
|---|---|---|---|---|---|---|---|---|---|---|---|---|
| 8 | | | | | | | | | | | | |
| 7 | | | | | | | | | | | | |
| 6 | | | | | | | | | | | | |
| 5 | | | | | | | | Grant | | | | |
| 4 | | | | | | | | Joe | | Val | | |
| 3 | Hayley | | | Beth | | Donna | Faith | Jenny | | Alex | Annie | |
| 2 | Greg | Pam | Tony | Tish | | Scott | Kelly | Ray | | Rich | Sherry | |
| 1 | Kevin | Cindy | Paul | John | Lynn | Donna | Mike | Josh | Sally | Lon | Angela | Calvin |

**Family Pets Venn Diagram**

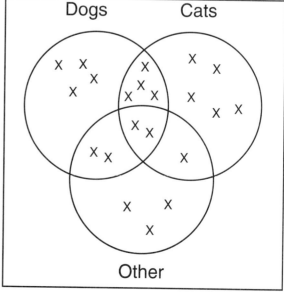

## Answer Key

1. skunks
2. ferrets
3. 19
4. monkeys
5. pythons
6. tigers
7. skunks

# Miss Petri's Class Pets

Complete the bar graph.
Use the information bank.
The first one is done for you.

### Information Bank

| | |
|---|---|
| white rats | 2 |
| hamsters | 8 |
| gerbils | 4 |
| rabbits | 6 |
| mice | 9 |
| guinea pigs | 3 |

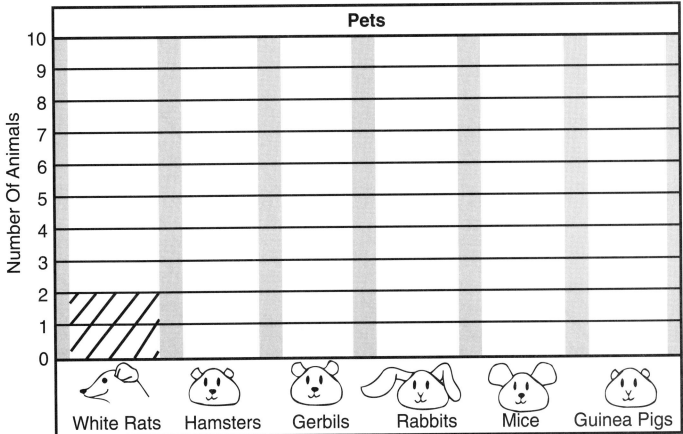

**Answer Key**

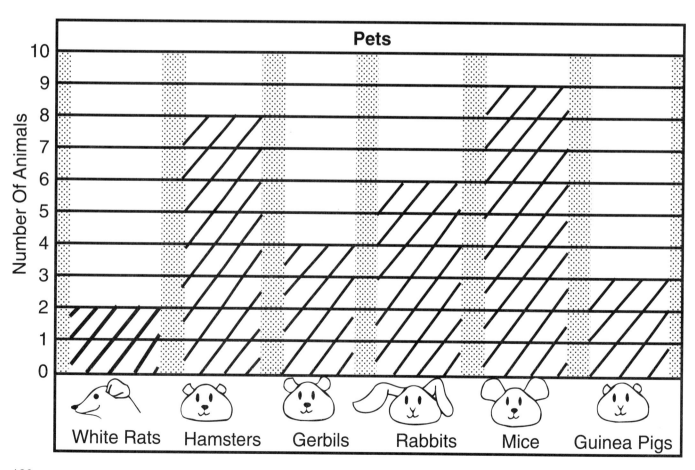

# Bunny Business

Listen carefully to the directions.
Use the graph.

J
I
H
G
F
E
D
C
B
A

1  2  3  4  5  6  7  8  9  10

## How To Use Page 121

Make a transparency of page 121. Project the transparency onto a wall or screen. Provide students with copies of page 121 and crayons. As you read the directions aloud to the students, illustrate each step on the projected transparency. Have students trace each step on their worksheets using a crayon. Then have students color and draw faces on their completed graph bunnies. Display graphic art worksheets on a bulletin board entitled "Bunny Business!"

## Variation

Duplicate the oral directions below, mount on tagboard, and laminate for durability. Place copies of page 121, directions, and a box of crayons at a center entitled "Bunny Business!" Have students complete bunny graphs during free or scheduled center time.

## Oral Directions

1. Put your crayon on the dot.
   Draw a line to connect:
2. C7 to B7
3. B7 to B5
4. B5 to A5
5. A5 to A2
6. A2 to B2
7. B2 to B3
8. B3 to D3
9. D3 to D2
10. D2 to H2
11. H2 to H1
12. H1 to J1
13. J1 to J2
14. J2 to I2
15. I2 to I3
16. I3 to G3
17. G3 to G4
18. G4 to I4
19. I4 to I5
20. I5 to J5
21. J5 to J6
22. J6 to H6
23. H6 to H5
24. H5 to F5
25. F5 to F8
26. F8 to E8
27. E8 to E9
28. E9 to D9
29. D9 to D10
30. D10 to C10
31. C10 to C9
32. C9 to A9
33. A9 to A6
34. A6 to B6

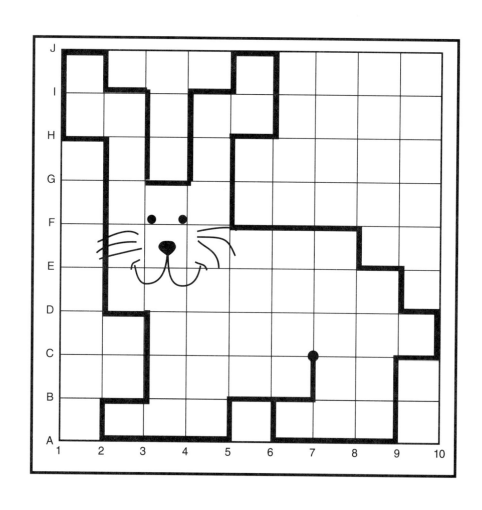

122

# Raining Cats And Dogs

Solve each fact.
Use the Color Code to color
the cats and dogs.

**Color Code**

| 0–10 | = | orange |
| 11–16 | = | yellow |
| 17–27 | = | brown |

2 x 5 = _____

3 x 5 = _____

1 x 2 = _____

2 x 6 = _____

3 x 6 = _____

3 x 9 = _____

3 x 4 = _____

2 x 7 = _____

2 x 8 = _____

1 x 1 = _____

1 x 5 = _____

2 x 2 = _____

2 x 3 = _____

3 x 7 = _____

0 x 7 = _____

3 x 8 = _____

0 x 8 = _____

2 x 4 = _____

3 x 3 = _____

2 x 9 = _____

**Bonus Box:** On the back of this sheet, list five things you like to do in the rain.

**Answer Key**

2 x 5 = 10 (O)

3 x 5 = 15 (Y)

1 x 2 = 2 (O)

2 x 6 = 12 (Y)

3 x 6 = 18 (B)

3 x 9 = 27 (B)

3 x 4 = 12 (Y)

2 x 8 = 16 (Y)

2 x 7 = 14 (Y)

1 x 1 = 1 (O)

1 x 5 = 5 (O)

2 x 2 = 4 (O)

2 x 3 = 6 (O)

3 x 7 = 21 (B)

0 x 7 = 0 (O)

3 x 8 = 24 (B)

0 x 8 = 0 (O)

2 x 4 = 8 (O)

3 x 3 = 9 (O)

2 x 9 = 18 (B)

Name _____

# Raindrops Keep Falling On My Head

Solve each fact.
Cut and glue the answer to match.

4
x 3
Glue.

1
x 3
Glue.

2
x 6
Glue.

4
x 7
Glue.

5
x 3
Glue.

5
x 4
Glue.

5
x 7
Glue.

4
x 4
Glue.

3
x 9
Glue.

5
x 5
Glue.

4
x 6
Glue.

4
x 8
Glue.

| 20 | 3 | 12 | 24 | 32 | 28 |

| 12 | 35 | 25 | 16 | 27 | 15 |

# How To Use Page 128

Duplicate a copy of page 128 for each of your students. Have each child attach her chart to the inside of a folder or to the top of her desk. As the child memorizes her multiplication facts, have her color the matching flowers.

**Answer Key
for page 125**

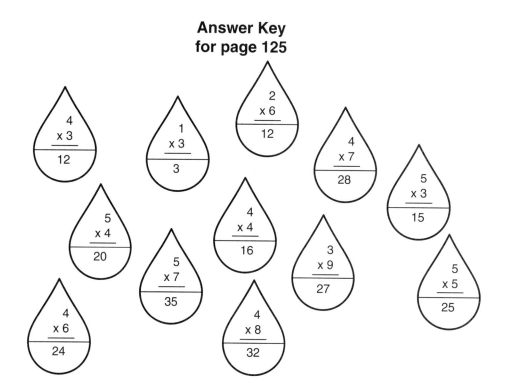

**Answer Key
for page 127**

**R.** 2 x 5 = 10        **C.** 7 x 4 = 28

**O.** 3 x 9 = 27        **D.** 9 x 9 = 81

**I.** 8 x 7 = 56        **A.** 4 x 1 = 4

**N.** 6 x 6 = 36        **W.** 8 x 8 = 64

**I.** 4 x 3 = 12        **U.** 5 x 5 = 25

**L.** 5 x 8 = 40        **H.** 7 x 6 = 42

**T.** 2 x 8 = 16        **Y.** 6 x 9 = 54

| C | L | O | U | D | Y | | W | I | T | H | | R | A | I | N |
|---|---|---|---|---|---|---|---|---|---|---|---|---|---|---|---|
| 28 | 40 | 27 | 25 | 81 | 54 | | 64 | 12 | 16 | 42 | | 10 | 4 | 56 | 36 |

Name _____

# Blame It On The Rain

Solve each problem.
To find today's forecast, match the letters to
    the numbered lines below.

## Today's Forecast

**R.**  2 x 5  =            **C.**  7 x 4  =

**O.**  3 x 9  =            **D.**  9 x 9  =

**I.**  8 x 7  =            **A.**  4 x 1  =

**N.**  6 x 6  =            **W.**  8 x 8  =

**I.**  4 x 3  =            **U.**  5 x 5  =

**L.**  5 x 8  =            **H.**  7 x 6  =

**T.**  2 x 8  =            **Y.**  6 x 9  =

28   40   27   25   81   54      64   12   16   42      10   4   56   36

**Bonus Box:** On a separate sheet of paper, predict the weather for your city or area for five days.
Next to each guess, write what the actual weather was. Were your predictions correct?

# Looks Like Rain!

When you memorize one of these multiplication fact families, color the matching flower.

# Singing In The Rain

Solve each problem.

| 8 | 6 | 2 | 9 | 3 | 4 | 5 | 7 |
|---|---|---|---|---|---|---|---|
| x 5 | x 8 | x 2 | x 8 | x 7 | x 1 | x 3 | x 8 |

| 8 | 4 | 6 | 2 | 7 | 9 | 3 | 7 |
|---|---|---|---|---|---|---|---|
| x 2 | x 4 | x 4 | x 3 | x 2 | x 4 | x 6 | x 1 |

| 5 | 6 | 3 | 7 | 4 | 6 | 7 | 4 |
|---|---|---|---|---|---|---|---|
| x 5 | x 0 | x 8 | x 7 | x 0 | x 6 | x 9 | x 2 |

| 6 | 8 | 5 | 4 | 6 | 4 | 3 | 5 |
|---|---|---|---|---|---|---|---|
| x 2 | x 4 | x 7 | x 7 | x 5 | x 9 | x 4 | x 8 |

**Bonus Box:** Write your own song to sing in the rain on the back of this sheet.

**Answer Key**

| | | | | | | | |
|---|---|---|---|---|---|---|---|
| 8<br>x 5<br>**40** | 6<br>x 8<br>**48** | 2<br>x 2<br>**4** | 9<br>x 8<br>**72** | 3<br>x 7<br>**21** | 4<br>x 1<br>**4** | 5<br>x 3<br>**15** | 7<br>x 8<br>**56** |
| 8<br>x 2<br>**16** | 4<br>x 4<br>**16** | 6<br>x 4<br>**24** | 2<br>x 3<br>**6** | 7<br>x 2<br>**14** | 9<br>x 4<br>**36** | 3<br>x 6<br>**18** | 7<br>x 1<br>**7** |
| 5<br>x 5<br>**25** | 6<br>x 0<br>**0** | 3<br>x 8<br>**24** | 7<br>x 7<br>**49** | 4<br>x 0<br>**0** | 6<br>x 6<br>**36** | 7<br>x 9<br>**63** | 4<br>x 2<br>**8** |
| 6<br>x 2<br>**12** | 8<br>x 4<br>**32** | 5<br>x 7<br>**35** | 4<br>x 7<br>**28** | 6<br>x 5<br>**30** | 4<br>x 9<br>**36** | 3<br>x 4<br>**12** | 5<br>x 8<br>**40** |

Multiplication: facts to 3

# Slalom Challenge

Look at each fact.
If the answer is correct, put a √ beside it.
If the answer is incorrect, put an X on it.

| $\begin{array}{r} 2 \\ \times 3 \\ \hline 6 \end{array}$ | | $\begin{array}{r} 9 \\ \times 3 \\ \hline 23 \end{array}$ | | | | $8 \times 1 = 8$ | | $5 \times 1 = 1$ |
|---|---|---|---|---|---|---|---|---|
| $9 \times 1 = 9$ | $\begin{array}{r} 6 \\ \times 0 \\ \hline 6 \end{array}$ | $4 \times 2 = 8$ | | $\begin{array}{r} 9 \\ \times 2 \\ \hline 18 \end{array}$ | | $\begin{array}{r} 6 \\ \times 3 \\ \hline 18 \end{array}$ | | |
| $\begin{array}{r} 5 \\ \times 2 \\ \hline 10 \end{array}$ | | $\begin{array}{r} 7 \\ \times 3 \\ \hline 21 \end{array}$ | | | | $7 \times 2 = 14$ | | |
| $4 \times 1 = 1$ | $\begin{array}{r} 10 \\ \times 2 \\ \hline 12 \end{array}$ | $6 \times 1 = 6$ | | $\begin{array}{r} 9 \\ \times 0 \\ \hline 9 \end{array}$ | | $\begin{array}{r} 4 \\ \times 3 \\ \hline 12 \end{array}$ | | $2 \times 2 = 4$ |
| $7 \times 0 = 0$ | $\begin{array}{r} 8 \\ \times 2 \\ \hline 16 \end{array}$ | $3 \times 0 = 0$ | | $\begin{array}{r} 3 \\ \times 3 \\ \hline 9 \end{array}$ | | | | |
| $\begin{array}{r} 8 \\ \times 3 \\ \hline 24 \end{array}$ | $5 \times 3 = 15$ | | | | | | | |
| $6 \times 2 = 12$ | $\begin{array}{r} 3 \\ \times 1 \\ \hline 3 \end{array}$ | | | | | | | |

Help Floyd find the right course. Color each box with a correct answer blue.

| **Bonus Box:** Write the correct answer beside each incorrect answer. |
|---|

## Extension Activity
## Multiplication Fact Wallet

Duplicate copies of the wallet pattern on page 134 onto white paper. Before handing out the patterns, cut the slits using an X-acto knife. Have students cut out the wallets along the bold line. Students then apply glue to the back, outside edges of their cutouts and fold them closed. Have students program the charts with the multiplication tables they are currently studying. Fold the wallet as shown, inserting the tab in the slit to close it. Color it as desired.

## Variation

Duplicate additional blank tables for students to program and staple inside their wallets. Students having difficulty with specific tables can use their wallets for reference.

## Materials Needed For Extension Activity

scissors
glue
pencils
crayons
X-acto knife

**Folded Wallet**

Sarah's
**Multiplication
Lifesaver**

| | | 2<br>x 3<br>—<br>6 ✓ | | 9<br>x 3<br>—<br>✗ 27 | | | |
|---|---|---|---|---|---|---|---|
| | | 9 x 1 = 9 ✓ | 6<br>x 0<br>—<br>✗ 0 | 4 x 2 = 8 ✓ | 9<br>x 2<br>—<br>18 ✓ | 8 x 1 = 8 ✓ | |
| 8<br>x 3<br>—<br>24 ✓ | 7 x 0 = 0 ✓ | 5<br>x 2<br>—<br>10 ✓ | | 7<br>x 3<br>—<br>21 ✓ | | 6<br>x 3<br>—<br>18 ✓ | 5 x 1 ✗ 5 |
| 6 x 2 = 12 ✓ | | 4 x 1 ✗ 4 | 10<br>x 2<br>—<br>✗ 20 | 6 x 1 = 6 ✓ | 9<br>x 0<br>—<br>✗ 0 | 7 x 2 = 14 ✓ | |
| 3<br>x 1<br>—<br>3 ✓ | 5 x 3 = 15 ✓ | 8<br>x 2<br>—<br>16 ✓ | 3 x 0 = 0 ✓ | 3<br>x 3<br>—<br>9 ✓ | | 4<br>x 3<br>—<br>12 ✓ | 2 x 2 = 4 ✓ |

# Different Strokes

Use the product pointers and the number lines.
Find the products.

$8 \times 4 = 32$

$$\begin{array}{r} 2 \\ \times 4 \\ \hline \end{array} \qquad \begin{array}{r} 5 \\ \times 5 \\ \hline \end{array} \qquad \begin{array}{r} 8 \\ \times 4 \\ \hline \end{array}$$

$$\begin{array}{r} 3 \\ \times 5 \\ \hline \end{array} \qquad \begin{array}{r} 6 \\ \times 4 \\ \hline \end{array} \qquad \begin{array}{r} 1 \\ \times 5 \\ \hline \end{array}$$

$0 \times 5 = $ _____

$7 \times 4 = $ _____

$9 \times 5 = $ _____

$1 \times 4 = $ _____

$$\begin{array}{r} 2 \\ \times 5 \\ \hline \end{array} \qquad \begin{array}{r} 0 \\ \times 4 \\ \hline \end{array} \qquad \begin{array}{r} 8 \\ \times 5 \\ \hline \end{array}$$

$$\begin{array}{r} 5 \\ \times 4 \\ \hline \end{array} \qquad \begin{array}{r} 6 \\ \times 5 \\ \hline \end{array} \qquad \begin{array}{r} 9 \\ \times 4 \\ \hline \end{array}$$

$4 \times 5 = $ _____

$3 \times 4 = $ _____

$7 \times 5 = $ _____

$4 \times 4 = $ _____

Slit.

x4

Slit.

x5

Fold. Gus

Fold. Gertie

product pointers

**Bonus Box:** On the back of this sheet, write the fours table through 15 x 4 and the fives table through 12 x 5. Use the product pointers to help you.

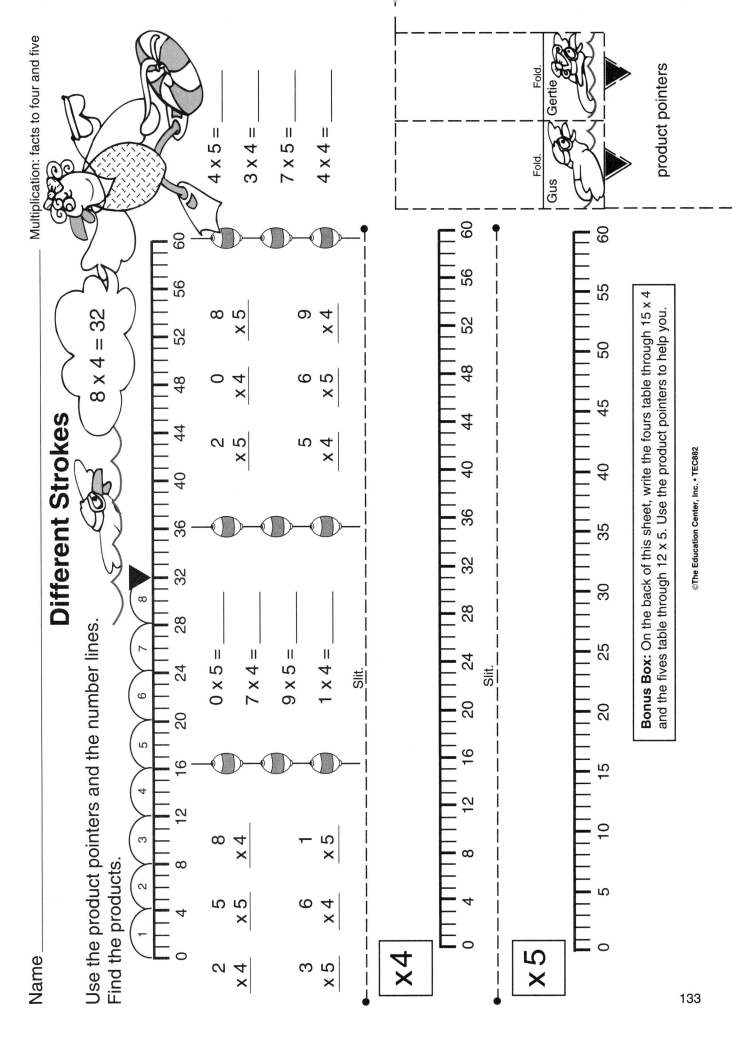

# How To Use Page 133

Duplicate copies of page 133 onto white construction paper. Before handing out the worksheets, cut the slits with an X-acto knife. Have students cut out Gus and Gertie and fold them to make pointers. Students insert the product pointers into the slits as shown. Then they manipulate the pointers as they work their facts.

## Materials Needed

scissors
X-acto knife

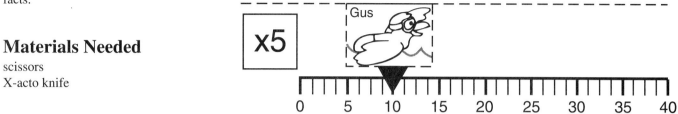

## Wallet Pattern

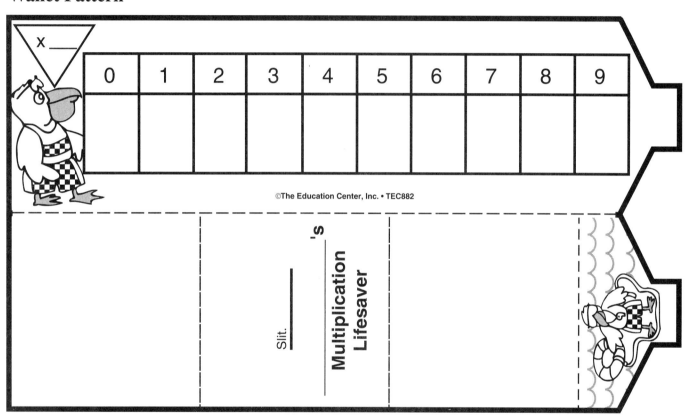

©The Education Center, Inc. • TEC882

Multiplication Lifesaver

Name _____

# Catch A Wave

Solve the problems.
Cross out each answer as you use it.

| 54 | 45 |
| 35 | 16 | 14 |
| 28 | 61 | 56 |

| 18 |
| 24 | 29 | 64 |
| 81 | 63 |
| 72 | 36 | 40 |
| 49 | 42 | 63 |

| 18 | 9 | 42 |
| 24 | 21 |
| 32 |

| 54 | 23 |
| 6 | 27 | 30 |
| 48 | 56 |
| 12 | 36 | 41 |

| 3 x 8 | 2 x 7 | 6 x 6 | 1 x 9 | 9 x 7 | 2 x 9 | 2 x 8 | 6 x 7 |

2 x 6 = ____    4 x 9 = ____    6 x 8 = ____    3 x 7 = ____

| 4 x 8 | 7 x 6 | 3 x 9 | 5 x 8 | 7 x 9 | 4 x 7 | 9 x 9 | 4 x 6 |

7 x 7 = ____    8 x 8 = ____    5 x 7 = ____    3 x 6 = ____

| 5 x 6 | 6 x 9 | 9 x 8 | 8 x 7 | 1 x 6 | 9 x 6 | 5 x 9 | 7 x 8 |

Percy will ride the wave that has all the answers crossed out.
Color the wave Percy will ride dark blue.
Color the other waves light blue.

©The Education Center, Inc. • TEC882

135

## Award

Duplicate copies of this award for students mastering two or more multiplication tables.

_____
Student

is making quite a

# splash

with
multiplication!

_____
Teacher

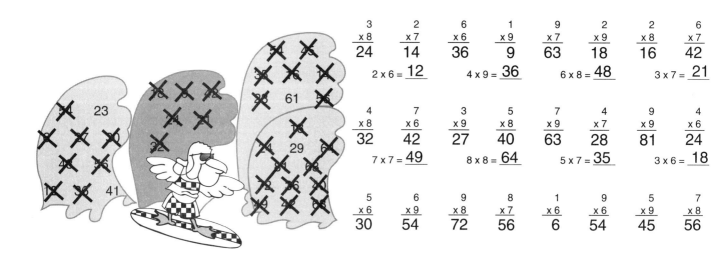

| | | | | | | |
|---|---|---|---|---|---|---|
| 3 x 8 = 24 | 2 x 7 = 14 | 6 x 6 = 36 | 1 x 9 = 9 | 9 x 7 = 63 | 2 x 9 = 18 | 2 x 8 = 16 | 6 x 7 = 42 |

2 x 6 = 12    4 x 9 = 36    6 x 8 = 48    3 x 7 = 21

| 4 x 8 = 32 | 7 x 6 = 42 | 3 x 9 = 27 | 5 x 8 = 40 | 7 x 9 = 63 | 4 x 7 = 28 | 9 x 9 = 81 | 4 x 6 = 24 |

7 x 7 = 49    8 x 8 = 64    5 x 7 = 35    3 x 6 = 18

| 5 x 6 = 30 | 6 x 9 = 54 | 9 x 8 = 72 | 8 x 7 = 56 | 1 x 6 = 6 | 9 x 6 = 54 | 5 x 9 = 45 | 7 x 8 = 56 |

# Hippity Hop To The Bakery Shop

**Start**

**Directions for 2 players:**

1. Stack the cards faceup.
2. Place your markers on Start.
3. In turn, draw a card and name the fraction that is shaded.
4. Turn the card over to check. If correct, move your marker to the nearest matching fraction. If incorrect, do not move. Then return the card to the bottom of the stack.
5. The first person to reach Finish wins!

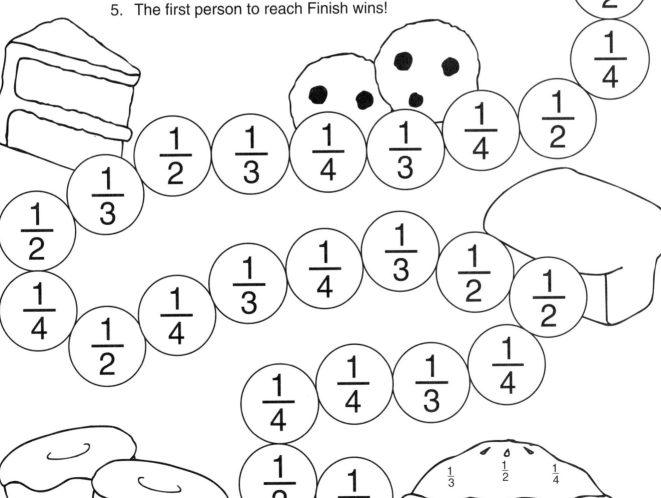

**Finish**

# How To Use This Unit (Pages 137–142)

After teaching lessons about halves, thirds, eighths, and fourths to your youngsters, use the game and skill sheets in this unit as entertaining reinforcement activities.

## How To Use Pages 137 And 138

Duplicate the gameboard on page 137 and the game cards and markers below on construction paper for each pair of students. Code the backs of the cards with fractions for self-checking and, if desired, laminate all of the game pieces for durability. Cut out the game cards and the markers. Have student pairs play the game according to the directions on the gameboard.

**Game markers**

**Game cards**

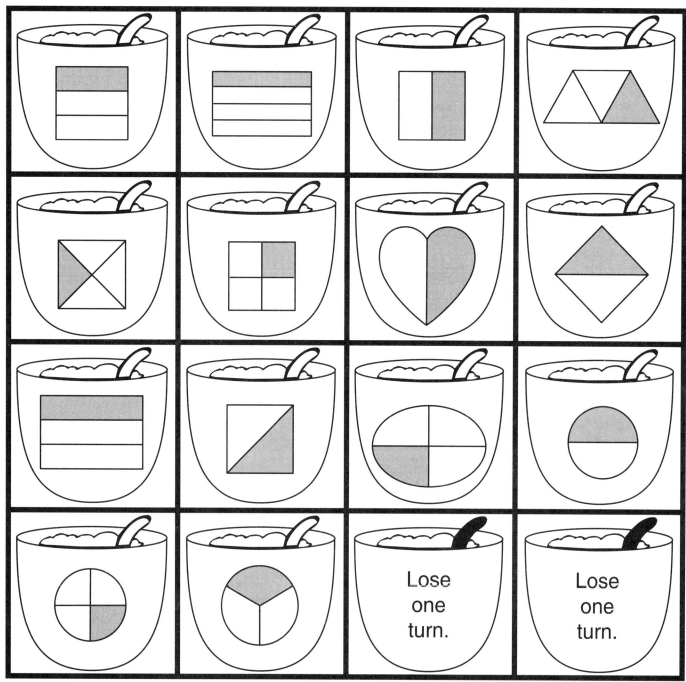

©The Education Center, Inc. • TEC882

Name _____

# We're Cooking Now!

Follow the directions.

Draw a hat on $\frac{1}{3}$ of the bakers.

Color $\frac{1}{4}$ of the spoons black.

Color $\frac{1}{2}$ of the cookies brown.

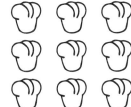

Circle $\frac{1}{3}$ of the rolls.

Draw nuts on $\frac{1}{3}$ of the brownies.

Color $\frac{1}{2}$ of the cakes yellow.

Draw sprinkles on $\frac{1}{4}$ of the cupcakes.

Color $\frac{1}{4}$ of the doughnuts orange.

Color $\frac{1}{3}$ of the donuts green.

Draw smiles on $\frac{1}{2}$ of the children.

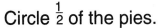

Circle $\frac{1}{2}$ of the pies.

Draw chips on $\frac{1}{4}$ of the cookies.

# Answer Key

(The pictures that are colored may vary, as long as the correct number is marked in each box.)

Draw a hat on $\frac{1}{3}$ of the bakers.

Color $\frac{1}{4}$ of the spoons black.

Color $\frac{1}{2}$ of the cookies brown.

Circle $\frac{1}{3}$ of the rolls.

Draw nuts on $\frac{1}{3}$ of the brownies.

Color $\frac{1}{2}$ of the cakes yellow.

Draw sprinkles on $\frac{1}{4}$ of the cupcakes.

Color $\frac{1}{4}$ of the doughnuts orange.

Color $\frac{1}{3}$ of the donuts green.

Draw smiles on $\frac{1}{2}$ of the children.

Circle $\frac{1}{2}$ of the pies.

Draw chips on $\frac{1}{4}$ of the cookies.

Name _____

# Baking Up A Storm

Cupcakes:

$1$   ○   $\frac{1}{2}$

$\frac{1}{2}$   ○   $\frac{1}{3}$

$\frac{1}{4}$   ○   $\frac{1}{2}$

$\frac{1}{3}$   ○   $\frac{1}{4}$

$\frac{3}{4}$   ○   $\frac{1}{4}$

$\frac{1}{2}$   ○   $\frac{3}{4}$

Write >, <, or = in each ○ .

$\frac{1}{4}$ ○ $\frac{1}{2}$

$\frac{2}{3}$ ○ $\frac{1}{3}$

$\frac{2}{4}$ ○ $\frac{1}{2}$

$\frac{2}{8}$ ○ $\frac{4}{8}$

$\frac{1}{4}$ ○ $\frac{2}{8}$

$\frac{3}{3}$ ○ $\frac{4}{4}$

$\frac{1}{4}$ ○ $\frac{1}{3}$

$\frac{2}{3}$ ○ $\frac{1}{8}$

$\frac{4}{8}$ ○ $\frac{1}{2}$

$\frac{3}{8}$ ○ $\frac{1}{2}$

141

# Extension Activity
## Fruit Pizzas

Making fruit pizzas is a delicious way to culminate your fractions unit. Divide your students into groups of five or six. To make a fruit pizza, each group needs one ready-to-eat pizza crust (Boboli pizza crusts work well) covered with a layer of whipped cream. Each group also needs an assortment of sliced fruits (such as bananas, strawberries, kiwis, blueberries, and pineapple) placed in separate containers, and several spoons.

Before making a pizza, have each group plan the arrangement of the fruit toppings. Give each group a construction-paper circle; then have students divide the circle into equal sections using crayons. Students discuss the fruit toppings desired for each section. Have a designated student from the group write the topping names in the appropriate sections. Students may choose to place more than one topping in a section. For example, students may decide to have bananas on half of the pizza, kiwi slices on a quarter of the pizza, and strawberries on three quarters of the pizza (partially overlapping the bananas).

When the group has planned its fruit pizza, allow students to place the fruit toppings on the pizza crust in the designated arrangement. Cover the pizzas with foil and freeze them for about an hour. While waiting for the pizzas to set, have the groups take turns sharing with their classmates about the fractional arrangements of their fruit pizzas. When the fruit pizzas are ready, slice them up and eat!

**Answer Key**

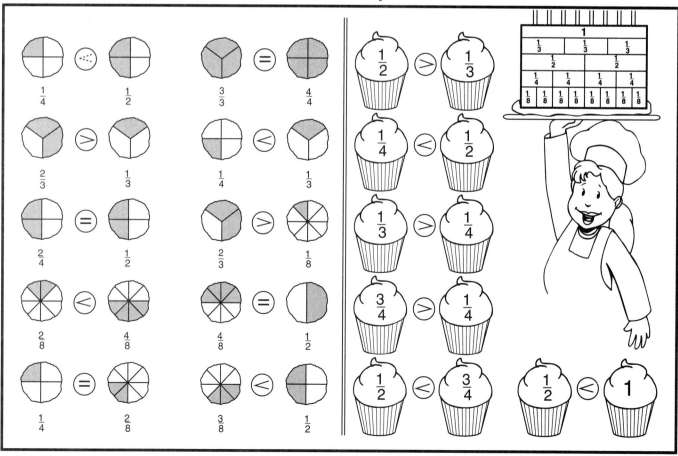

Name_____

# Take Off With Fractions

Look at the circles inside the hot-air balloon. Color all the halves **red**.
Color all the thirds **blue**. Color all the fourths **yellow**.

**Bonus Box:** Give your
hot-air balloon a name.
Describe what you think
it would feel like to take
a trip in a hot-air balloon.

# Background For The Teacher
## Hot Air Balloons

Ballooning started in the late 1700s with two brothers from France, Jacques Étienne and Joseph Montgolfier. They experimented by filling small paper bags with smoke. (They thought the smoke made the balloon rise!) In September 1783, they sent up a duck, a rooster, and a sheep in the world's first hot-air balloon ride. On October 15, 1783, Jean Francois Pilâtre de Rozier, a French scientist, was the first person to take an anchored balloon ride. One month later on November 21, Pilâtre de Rozier and an army officer made the first free flight. They stayed airborne for 25 minutes.

On the ground, a pilot spreads out a nylon or polyester balloon which is attached to a wicker or aluminum basket. A big fan blows air into the opening, or mouth, of the balloon. When the balloon is half-inflated, the pilot starts a small propane burner and heats the air inside the balloon. The air expands inside the balloon and inflates it. Then the balloon lifts off. Dynamics of flight are simple: to ascend, the pilot burns more gas; to descend, the pilot burns less. If a quick descent is necessary, the pilot opens the cooling vent (a crown-shaped vent toward the top of the balloon) by pulling a cord.

Ballooning has quickly become a trend, especially in Europe. Currently there are many balloon rallies both in the United States and Europe. There are more than 2,000 sport balloonists in the United States today. Indianola, Iowa, hosts the annual U.S. National Hot-Air Balloon Championships.

# Extension Activities
## Fractions

— Using only one color of poster board, cut out several circles, squares, and rectangles. Cut each shape into halves, thirds, or fourths. Have students put the whole units back together. As students become proficient with these fractional parts, add fifths, sixths, and eighths. For younger students, make the whole units out of different colors.

— Use tongue depressors divided into fractional parts to help students recognize halves, thirds, fourths, fifths, and sixths. Color the fractional parts with felt pens. Print answers on the backs to make the activity self-correcting.

— Make a game of fraction Concentration out of tagboard cards. Have matching sets of cards equal one whole unit. For example, one card will show one-third and the matching card will show two-thirds. Use pictures, sets, or numerals. Students try to match a complete unit to win the card pair and another turn.

— Provide students with the opportunity to practice recognizing fractions. On the front of a tagboard flash card, illustrate a proper fraction. On the back of the same card, write the fraction in numeral form. These cards can be used by two students as a game, or by the teacher with the whole class.

## Answer Key

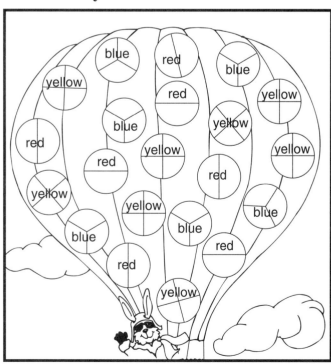

# Ring Around The Balloon

Look at the shapes inside the balloons.
Circle the fraction that tells how much of the shape is shaded.

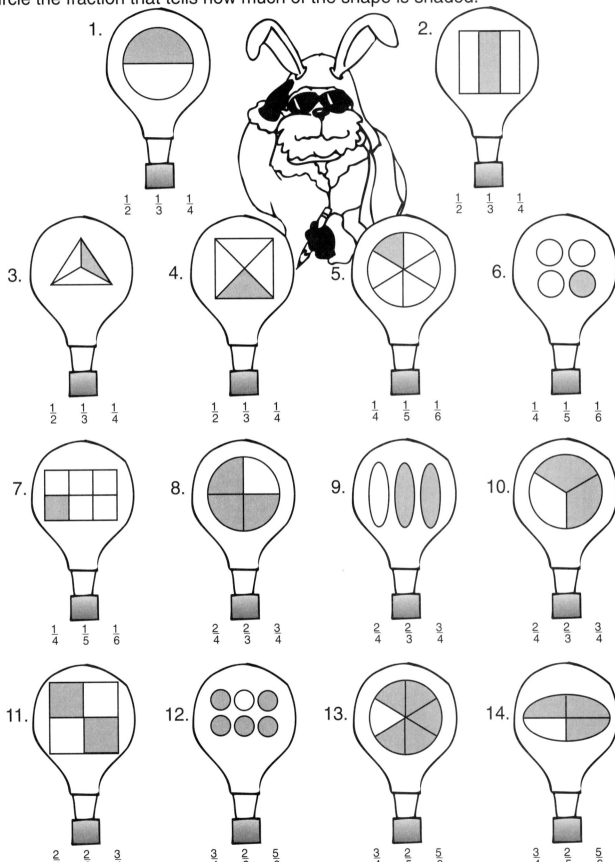

1. $\frac{1}{2}$  $\frac{1}{3}$  $\frac{1}{4}$

2. $\frac{1}{2}$  $\frac{1}{3}$  $\frac{1}{4}$

3. $\frac{1}{2}$  $\frac{1}{3}$  $\frac{1}{4}$

4. $\frac{1}{2}$  $\frac{1}{3}$  $\frac{1}{4}$

5. $\frac{1}{4}$  $\frac{1}{5}$  $\frac{1}{6}$

6. $\frac{1}{4}$  $\frac{1}{5}$  $\frac{1}{6}$

7. $\frac{1}{4}$  $\frac{1}{5}$  $\frac{1}{6}$

8. $\frac{2}{4}$  $\frac{2}{3}$  $\frac{3}{4}$

9. $\frac{2}{4}$  $\frac{2}{3}$  $\frac{3}{4}$

10. $\frac{2}{4}$  $\frac{2}{3}$  $\frac{3}{4}$

11. $\frac{2}{4}$  $\frac{2}{3}$  $\frac{3}{4}$

12. $\frac{3}{4}$  $\frac{2}{3}$  $\frac{5}{6}$

13. $\frac{3}{4}$  $\frac{2}{5}$  $\frac{5}{6}$

14. $\frac{3}{4}$  $\frac{2}{5}$  $\frac{5}{6}$

# Gondola Pattern

Reproduce gondola pattern for students.
To construct gondola:

1. Color pattern piece to look like a basket.
2. Cut out gondola on solid lines.
3. Make folds on dotted lines.
4. Glue Tab A to B to make a square.
5. Fold down bottom of the basket and glue.

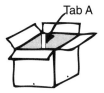 

Blow up balloon and tie off. Attach four 6-inch-long strings to the balloon and to circles on each side of the gondola. Toss the balloon in the air and watch it float down. See what kind of scientific observations your students can make!

## Answer Key

| | | | |
|---|---|---|---|
| 1. 1/2 | | 9. 2/3 |
| 2. 1/3 | | 10. 2/3 |
| 3. 1/3 | | 11. 2/4 |
| 4. 1/4 | | 12. 5/6 |
| 5. 1/6 | | 13. 5/6 |
| 6. 1/4 | | 14. 3/4 |
| 7. 1/6 | | |
| 8. 3/4 | | |

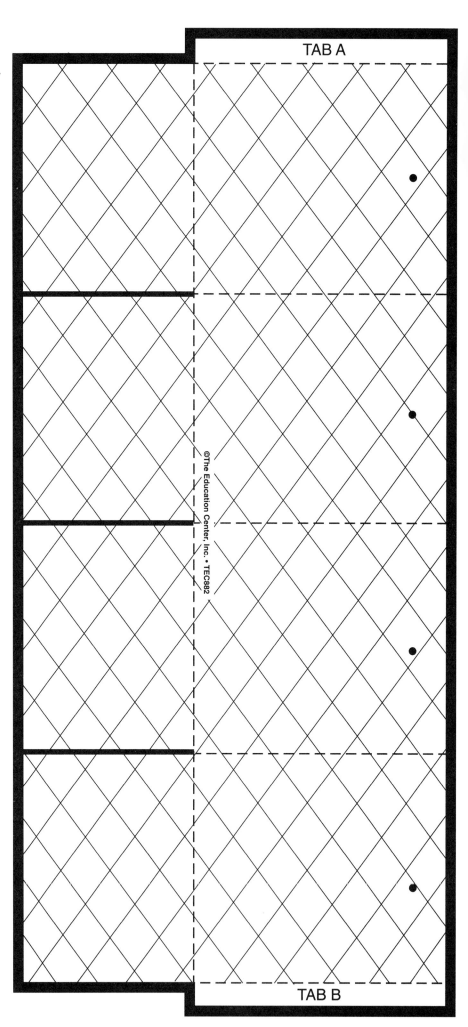

TAB A

TAB A

TAB B

Name_____

# Flying High With Fractions

Write the fraction for each shaded part in the balloon basket.
Cross out your answer in the answer bank.
There will be one answer left over.

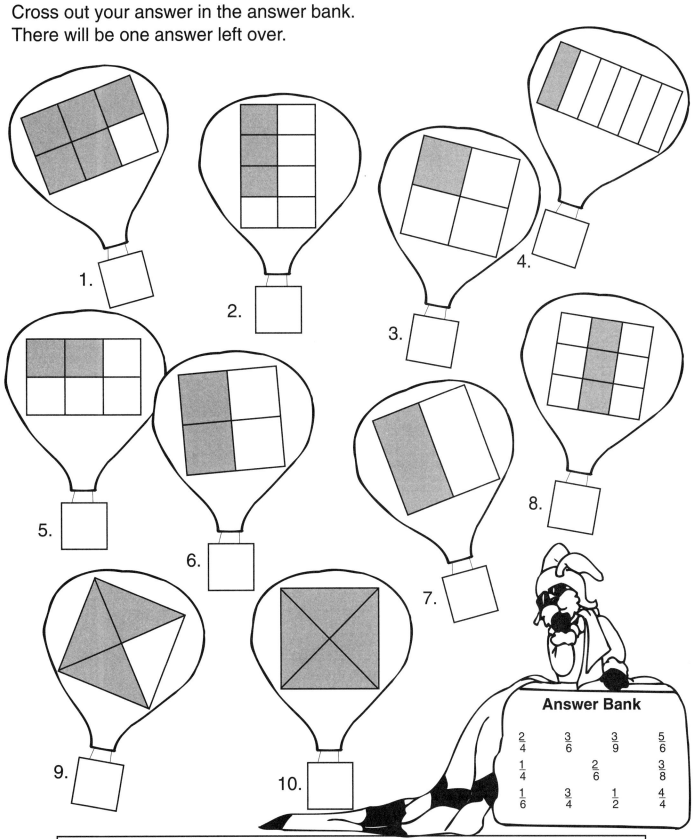

**Answer Bank**

$\frac{2}{4}$   $\frac{3}{6}$   $\frac{3}{9}$   $\frac{5}{6}$

$\frac{1}{4}$   $\frac{2}{6}$   $\frac{3}{8}$

$\frac{1}{6}$   $\frac{3}{4}$   $\frac{1}{2}$   $\frac{4}{4}$

**Bonus Box:** Try to divide a square so that it has ten equal parts. What fraction would each part be?

# Hot-Air Balloon Pattern

Reproduce the hot-air balloon pattern for each student. Have each student choose a fraction and show it by dividing and shading the center circle to represent this fraction. Then students can color the hot-air balloon and add a square for the gondola. Attach brightly colored ribbon to the balloon and gondola. Display on a bulletin board with the heading "Flying High With Fractions."

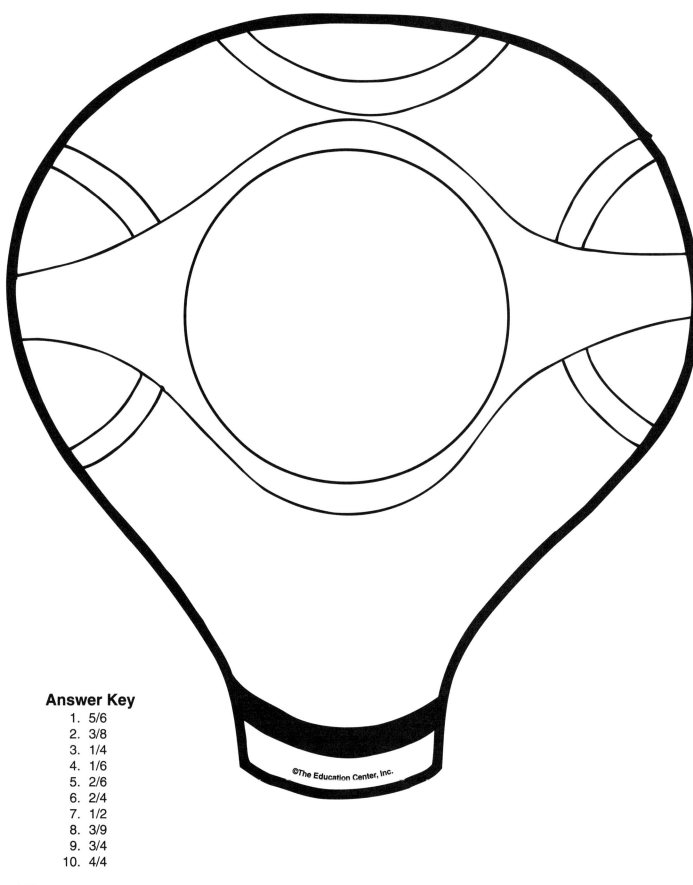

©The Education Center, Inc.

**Answer Key**

1. 5/6
2. 3/8
3. 1/4
4. 1/6
5. 2/6
6. 2/4
7. 1/2
8. 3/9
9. 3/4
10. 4/4

Name

# Balloon Bonanza

Help Buster decorate the balloons. Look at the balloons below and color the fractional parts.

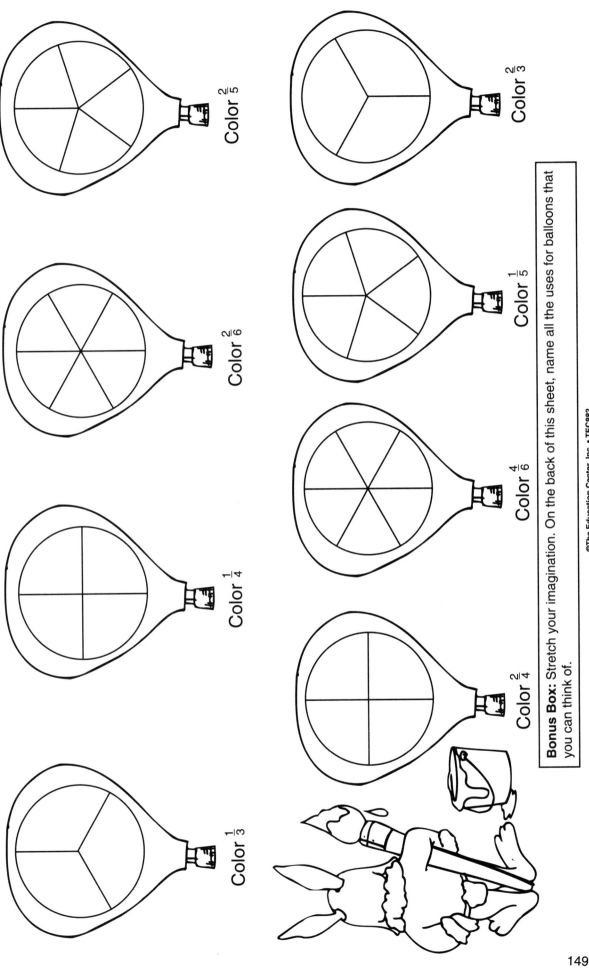

Color $\frac{1}{3}$

Color $\frac{1}{4}$

Color $\frac{2}{6}$

Color $\frac{2}{5}$

Color $\frac{2}{4}$

Color $\frac{4}{6}$

Color $\frac{1}{5}$

Color $\frac{2}{3}$

**Bonus Box:** Stretch your imagination. On the back of this sheet, name all the uses for balloons that you can think of.

149

## Follow-up Activity

Duplicate a copy of the award below for those students
who show progress with fractions.

# Up, Up, And Away

**Student**

## is soaring
## with fractions!

**Teacher**

**Date**

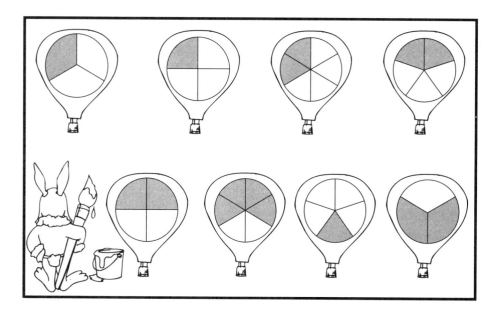

(Answers may vary.)

# Pickin' Watermelon

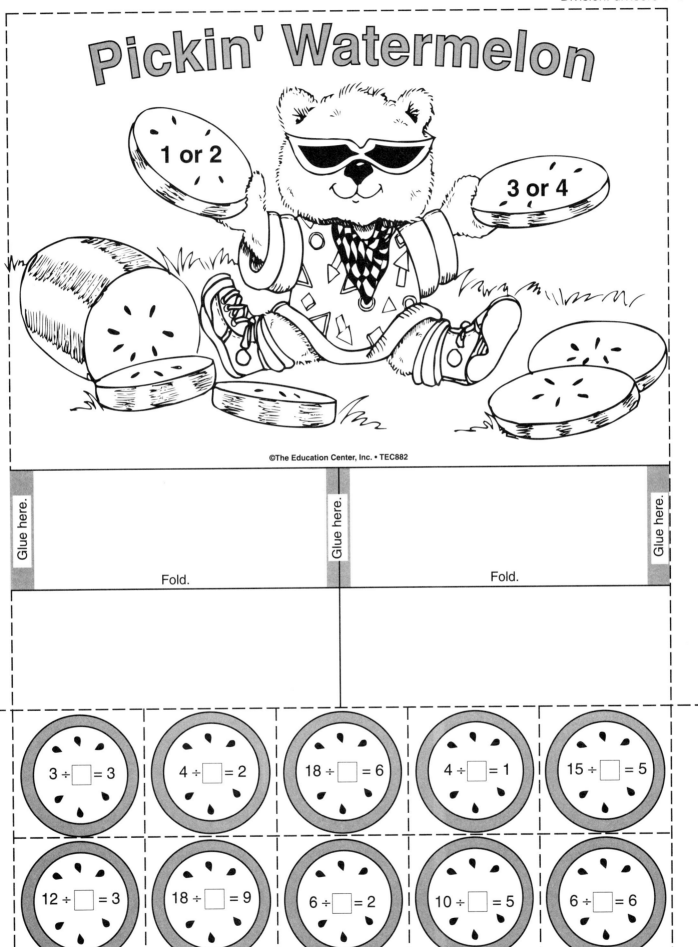

1 or 2

3 or 4

©The Education Center, Inc. • TEC882

Glue here.

Glue here.

Glue here.

Fold.

Fold.

$3 \div \square = 3$

$4 \div \square = 2$

$18 \div \square = 6$

$4 \div \square = 1$

$15 \div \square = 5$

$12 \div \square = 3$

$18 \div \square = 9$

$6 \div \square = 2$

$10 \div \square = 5$

$6 \div \square = 6$

151

# Directions For The Students (Page 151)

1. Cut out along the dotted lines.
2. Fold and glue along the lines as shown.
3. Complete each division fact.
4. Place the division fact in the correct pocket.

## Variations

— White out the divisors and the division facts on the watermelon slices before duplicating. Program with other math facts or language-arts skills.

— Duplicate, color, and laminate the worksheet. Cut out the components and staple on the glue lines. Store the components in a press-on pocket attached to the back. Add the directions: "Complete the division facts with a wipe-off crayon. Place the facts in the correct pockets. Check with the answer key." Include an answer key for self-checking. Place the activity in a math center for individual practice.

## Extension Activities
## Division

— You'll slice up some hands-on division practice your students are sure to enjoy with this idea! Provide a watermelon, sharp knife, large platter, plastic bags, and napkins. Cut the watermelon into slices and place on the platter. Take the slices, plastic bags, napkins, and your class outside and enjoy this tasty treat in the sunshine. Have the students place their watermelon seeds in the plastic bags. Once inside, wash and dry the watermelon seeds. Distribute the dry seeds to the students. List division problems on the chalkboard. Then, as a class, have the students manipulate their seeds to work the division problems. For extra practice, demonstrate the problems by manipulating the seeds atop an overhead projector.

— Your students will want to practice their division facts when you make these tempting watermelon flash cards! Duplicate copies of the watermelon slice pattern (on page 154) onto red construction paper. Trim the edges with a green crayon to create the rinds. Then, using a black marker, program the slices with division facts and answers as shown. Laminate for durability and cut out. Store the flash cards in a zippered bag at your math center.

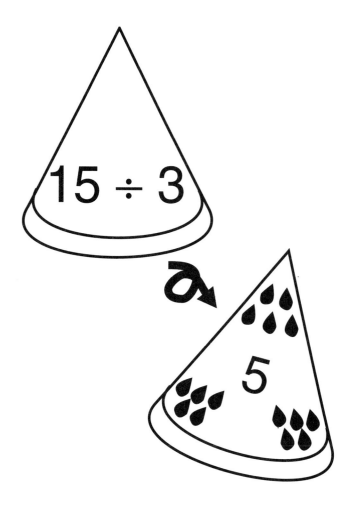

## Answer Key
### 1 or 2
$3 \div \boxed{1} = 3$
$4 \div \boxed{2} = 2$
$18 \div \boxed{2} = 9$
$10 \div \boxed{2} = 5$
$6 \div \boxed{1} = 6$

### 3 or 4
$18 \div \boxed{3} = 6$
$4 \div \boxed{4} = 1$
$15 \div \boxed{3} = 5$
$12 \div \boxed{4} = 3$
$6 \div \boxed{3} = 2$

152

Name _____

# A Scrumptious Slice!

Solve the problems.
Color by the code.

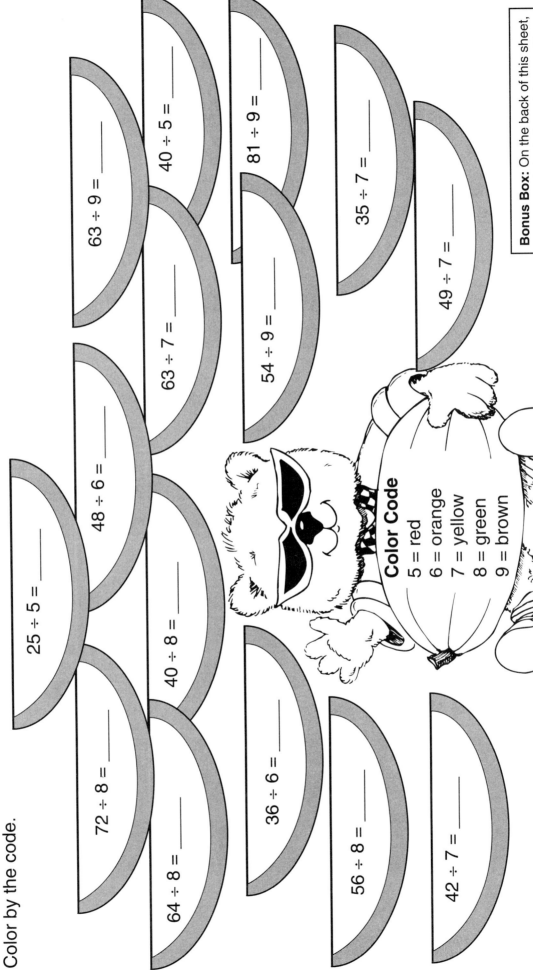

25 ÷ 5 = ____

48 ÷ 6 = ____

63 ÷ 9 = ____

40 ÷ 5 = ____

63 ÷ 7 = ____

81 ÷ 9 = ____

54 ÷ 9 = ____

35 ÷ 7 = ____

49 ÷ 7 = ____

72 ÷ 8 = ____

40 ÷ 8 = ____

64 ÷ 8 = ____

36 ÷ 6 = ____

56 ÷ 8 = ____

42 ÷ 7 = ____

**Color Code**
5 = red
6 = orange
7 = yellow
8 = green
9 = brown

**Bonus Box:** On the back of this sheet, change each fact above into a multiplication fact.

©The Education Center, Inc. • TEC882

153

# Pattern

Use this pattern with the extension activity on page 152.

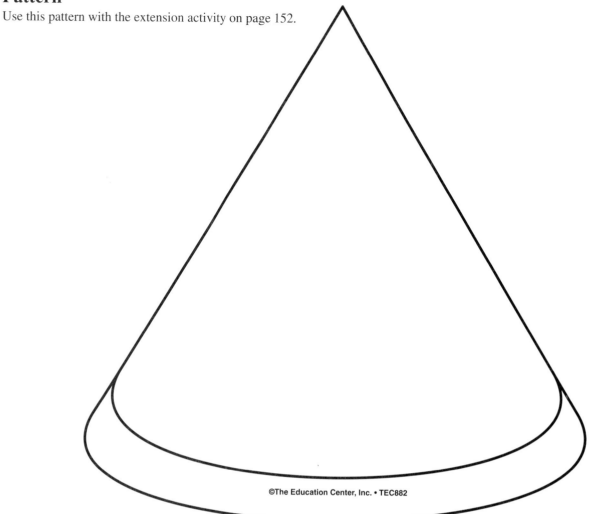

©The Education Center, Inc. • TEC882

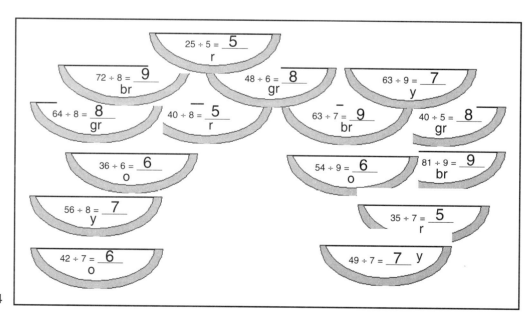

25 ÷ 5 = __5__
r

72 ÷ 8 = __9__
br

48 ÷ 6 = __8__
gr

63 ÷ 9 = __7__
y

64 ÷ 8 = __8__
gr

40 ÷ 8 = __5__
r

63 ÷ 7 = __9__
br

40 ÷ 5 = __8__
gr

36 ÷ 6 = __6__
o

54 ÷ 9 = __6__
o

81 ÷ 9 = __9__
br

56 ÷ 8 = __7__
y

35 ÷ 7 = __5__
r

42 ÷ 7 = __6__
o

49 ÷ 7 = __7__ y

Name _____

# Patch Of Facts

Complete each fact.
Cross off a leaf as you use the corresponding number.

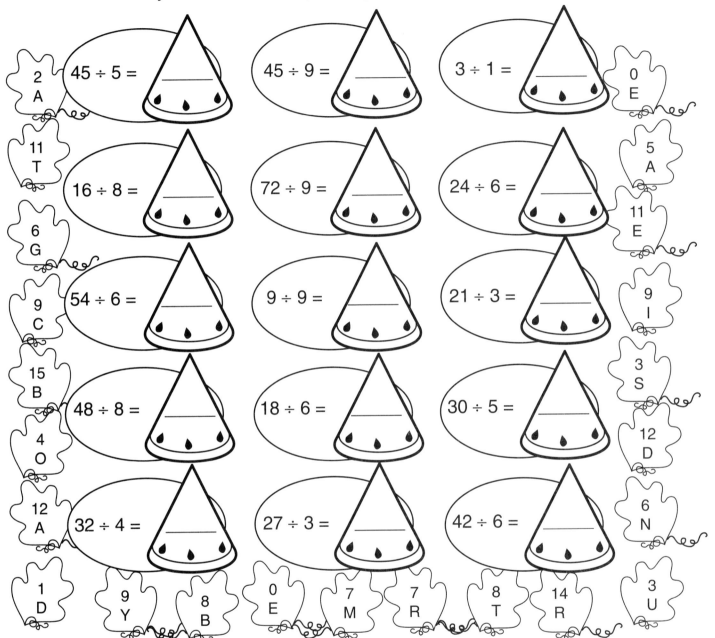

2 A

11 T

6 G

9 C

15 B

4 O

12 A

45 ÷ 5 = _____

16 ÷ 8 = _____

54 ÷ 6 = _____

48 ÷ 8 = _____

32 ÷ 4 = _____

45 ÷ 9 = _____

72 ÷ 9 = _____

9 ÷ 9 = _____

18 ÷ 6 = _____

27 ÷ 3 = _____

3 ÷ 1 = _____

24 ÷ 6 = _____

21 ÷ 3 = _____

30 ÷ 5 = _____

42 ÷ 6 = _____

0 E

5 A

11 E

9 I

3 S

12 D

6 N

1 D    9 Y    8 B    0 E    7 M    7 R    8 T    14 R    3 U

On the lines below, write the letters from the leaves that were not crossed off.

___ ___ ___ ___ ___ ___ ___ ___

Unscramble the letters to find out who has been eating the watermelons in
Farmer John's patch.
Write your answer in the blanks.

___ ___ ___ . ___ ___ ___ ___

# Award

Reproduce this award for any student showing progress in division fact skills.

No matter how you slice it...

_____
Name

knows the division facts!

©The Education Center, Inc.

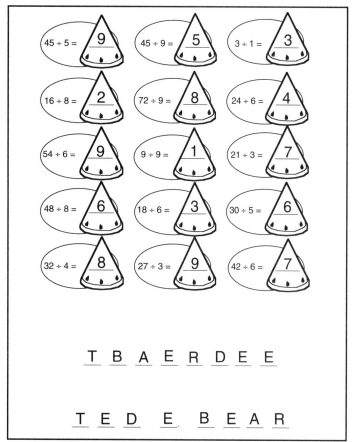

$45 \div 5 =$ 9  $45 \div 9 =$ 5  $3 \div 1 =$ 3

$16 \div 8 =$ 2  $72 \div 9 =$ 8  $24 \div 6 =$ 4

$54 \div 6 =$ 9  $9 \div 9 =$ 1  $21 \div 3 =$ 7

$48 \div 8 =$ 6  $18 \div 6 =$ 3  $30 \div 5 =$ 6

$32 \div 4 =$ 8  $27 \div 3 =$ 9  $42 \div 6 =$ 7

T B A E R D E E

T E D E   B E A R

156

Name _____

# Smooth Sailing

Use a calculator.
Find what is missing in each math sentence.
Hint: Use the +, −, x, or number keys.
Write it in the box.

3 □ 9 = 27

□ x 2 = 12

□ + 6 = 14

7 □ 2 = 14

2 x □ = 16

6 □ 1 = 6

8 x □ = 56

9 □ 6 = 3

□ x 5 = 25

4 □ 0 = 0

6 + □ = 13

9 □ 7 = 16

6 x 5 = □

21 □ 9 = 12

5 + □ = 13

Be sure to clear your calculator after each problem!

6 □ 4 = 24          □ + 9 = 14          14 □ 8 = 6

7 x □ = 28          3 □ 9 = 12

Unscramble the letters to find:
1. where Christopher Columbus was born

    YAITL _____
2. where Christopher Columbus's voyage began

    INASP _____

# Background For The Teacher
## Christopher Columbus

Christopher Columbus (1451–1506) has gone down in history as the discoverer of America even though Native Americans had lived in North and South America for thousands of years. The reason is due to the fact that Europeans at that time were unaware of the existence of North and South America and so it *was* a discovery to them. Columbus was not trying to prove that the world was round since this was already a known fact. His plan was to find a short route to the Indies. Columbus thought he could sail west along the latitudes of the Canary Islands to reach a group of islands near Japan where natives would accept him as lord and master. He hoped to build a great trading center for products for both the East and West.

Columbus presented his plan to King John II of Portugal, but the king was not interested. He later appealed to King Ferdinand and Queen Isabella of Spain for support. The Spanish royalty not only gave Columbus ships, a crew, and supplies, but also agreed to give him a noble rank, the title of admiral, a governorship of any lands he discovered, and a large share in any future treasures and trade.

On August 3, 1492, Columbus set sail from Palos, Spain, with three ships named the *Santa María,* the *Niña,* and the *Pinta.* Columbus sighted land at 2 A.M. on October 12, 1492. It was an island in the Bahamas he named San Salvador. As Columbus landed on the beach, he still believed that he had found the islands of the Indies, near Japan. With such a belief, Columbus named the people on this island "Indians" and the islands the "West Indies." The explorer did not find a land filled with gold but did find the natives smoking tobacco. He was the first to expose Europeans to tobacco.

The *Santa María* was wrecked on a reef on Christmas Eve, and the voyage home was a rough one for the two remaining ships. He reported his discovery to Ferdinand and Isabella, and they honored their pledge to him. Columbus made three more voyages to the New World in the years to come. On his first and second voyages, Columbus explored the coasts of Cuba, Hispaniola, Jamaica, and Puerto Rico. On his third and fourth voyages, he explored the mainland of South and Central America.

Even though Columbus was incorrect in his assumptions, his voyages changed the course of history. The New World, particularly America, was opened to settlement by Europeans in the years to come. Columbus has to be credited with being a great sailor as well. He found his way back and forth between the New World and Spain. This was no easy feat at a time of few navigational aids. The first voyage of Columbus has been celebrated annually on October 12 since 1920. Columbus Day became a national holiday in 1971 and is now celebrated on the second Monday in October in the United States.

**Answer Key**

1. Italy
2. Spain

Name _____

# Be A Calculator Champ!

Use a calculator to solve each problem.
Write the answer on the calculator's display screen.
Hint: Push ☐C (clear) after each problem.

1. 4 + 5 =      2. 2 + 6 =      3. 7 − 3 =

4. 8 − 4 = [_____] C      10. 9 − 7 = [_____] C

5. 6 + 7 = [_____] C      11. 8 + 8 = [_____] C

6. 5 + 9 = [_____] C      12. 8 − 3 = [_____] C

7. 9 − 3 = [_____] C      13. 9 + 3 = [_____] C

8. 7 + 8 = [_____] C      14. 7 − 2 = [_____] C

9. 6 − 6 = [_____] C      15. 4 + 3 = [_____] C

**Bonus Box:** Sammy Squirrel needs help counting nuts. Write five addition problems on the back of this sheet. Exchange papers with a partner. Solve the problems. Use a calculator.

## Extension Activities
## Calculators

— Establish a weekly "calculator day" for students to use calculators during math class. Possible uses of calculators in the classroom are endless. Here is a list of activities to get you started:

— Have student pairs exchange and correct their partners' papers using calculators.

— Give students math worksheets having correct and incorrect answers. Have students use calculators to find the teacher's mistakes.

— Provide students with math problems without signs (9 □ 6 = 3). Have students use the calculators to determine the missing signs.

— Allow students to complete difficult problems using calculators.

— Enlarge the calculator pattern below and make a transparency. Place the transparency on the overhead projector and have students "push the buttons" as their peers compute problems at their desks.

— Give student pairs flash cards and calculators. Students take turns showing the flash cards while their partners compute the answers.

**Pattern**

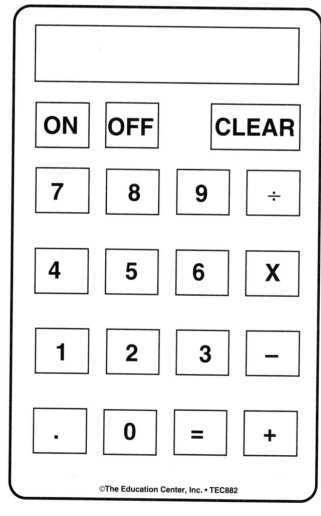

**Answer Key**
1. 9
2. 8
3. 4
4. 4
5. 13
6. 14
7. 6
8. 15
9. 0
10. 2
11. 16
12. 5
13. 12
14. 5
15. 7